Remember Me Young

Library of Congress Cataloging-in-Publication Data

Luso, Cecelia Tumminello de, 1937-
  Remember me young : Sicilian life beyond the veil / Cecelia Tumminello De Luso.
    pages cm
  Includes bibliographical references and index.
    ISBN 1-881901-94-7 (pbk. : alk. paper) 1. Luso, Cecelia Tumminello de, 1937- 2. Italian American women--New York (State)--New York--Biography. 3. Brooklyn (New York, N.Y.)--Biography. 4. Italian American families--New York (State)--New York. 5. Williamsburg (New York, N.Y.)--Social life and customs--20th century. 6. Bushwick (New York, N.Y.)--Social life and customs--20th century. 7. Brooklyn (New York, N.Y.)--Social life and customs--20th century. 8. New York (N.Y.)--Social life and customs--20th century. 9. Sicily (Italy)--Emigration and immigration--Biography. 10. United States--Emigration and immigration--Biography. I. Title.
  F128.9.I8L87 2013
  974.7'23043--dc23
                                2013018770

Acknowledgements

The publisher is grateful to Arba Sicula for a generous grant that in part made the publication of this book possible.

For information and for orders,write to:

Legas

P.O. Box 149
Brooklyn, NewYork
11204, USA

3 Wood Aster Bay
Ottawa, Ontario
K2R 1D3 Canada

Legaspublishing.com

Cecelia Tumminello De Luso

Remember Me Young

Sicilian Life Beyond the Veil

LEGAS

"*Un miliuni di grazzii a Gaetano Cipolla*, who is known for his indefatigable devotion to the preservation of the Sicilian Language and Culture."

Acknowledgements

To my brother Frank, without you reminiscing and telling us your version, writing this book would not have been as much fun.

To my husband Victor, thank you for the encouragement and saying, "Amazing, the vivid pictures you paint with words draws me into the stories." My children and their mates, thank you for enjoying. Carolyn, thank you for your sage advice from inception to the conclusion of this book.

My grandchildren, Nicholas, Karina, Vincent, Ryan, Brandon and Isabella thank you for not rolling your eyes or telling me you had to wash your dog, Scooter.

To my relatives, friends, teachers and classmates in the Long Island Writers' Guild, and Poets and Writers Society and Watercolor Classes past and present, without you I would not be me. . . Thank You. . .

Appreciation to Marion Campagna for the shared laughter recounting Sicilian proverbs.

Life's Map

Why do I wait?
Why do I ponder?
Leaves burst forth with no regard to old branches
Birds build nests with full anticipation of new life
Crocus and daffodils shake off the last of winter's ice crystals
Why do I wait?
Why do I ponder?
What I must see to feel alive, I wonder as I wander
Once when young I jumped right in
Now whispers from phantoms and ghosts I hear ... Too old,
too late! What for?
In my hands held tight, a map of life, creased and old I unfold
Roads well traveled, marked and worn, hills, mountain tops,
deep dark valleys I explored
And yet I see so much more for me to travel
When young I jumped right in, encouragement and assurance came
from within
Anger rises, face gets flushed, I stamp my foot,
Eyes grow wild and realize I'm neither a ghost nor a phantom
With a burst of youthful exuberance I jump
As I soar above the clouds, I feel my hands wide open
Goodbye life's map, come what may As I smile today. . .

Table of Contents

8

Introduction

To say I was born and raised in Brooklyn, New York, is the same as saying I come from the planet Earth. Only when you specify the neighborhood you came from, can you be understood.

Friends of mine came from Bay Ridge and Bensonhurst, where they enjoyed walking along 18th Avenue, visiting the small mom and pop shops. Walking along 86th Street, they would shop for gifts. Perhaps a big puffy baby blanket for the navy blue coach carriage. *La Patrina*, godmother shopped for the special long christening gown, which was worn by both girls and boys. They never missed a short stop at the Caffè Mille Luci or picking up the special cakes and little marzipan lamb for Pasqua from Alba Bakery. Along 17th Avenue on Sunday, you would smell "The Sauce". They smile remembering the Monsignor who did not like to hear the jingle of coins in the collection plate.

East New York was great, recollection as a teenager going to Saint Rita Roman Catholic Church and Saint Fortunata during their annual feast filled with music, food, and games of chance was exciting. Because I traveled by train to Franklin K. Lane High School, my friends were all from the surrounding area. Going to Rockaway Beach and Playland was just a ride on the bus. Shopping, of course, was done on Fulton Street in Downtown Brooklyn.

I belong to two neighborhoods: Williamsburg is where my mother's family lived forever; this was the area that taught me to love being a Sicilian. Identity was never an issue. My brother Frank and I absorbed into our own moral fiber the strong family trust and respect for others. We enjoyed the unconditional love from our parents, Mamma, aunt Anna, uncle Lorenzo, uncle Jimmy and aunt Lena.

Williamsburg was a cauldron bubbling over with Sicilian holiday joy, folklore, and proverbs from the past. There was a thin veil trying to cover the corruption and rape, sour secrets affecting us all. And then there was "The Love Story of Anna and Lorenzo."

Americanization was my mother's goal. We moved to the Bushwick section of Brooklyn. Here, we were surrounded with many nationalities. None of them spoke Italian or Sicilian. They were friendly, reserved and spoke only English. Here, we could participate fully in the broader society with no loss of ethnic identity or our ideals.

Itch and Scratch

Earliest recollection, what brings it to mind? Just idle chatter and women's talk brought back times we spent storing our woolen clothes with moth balls and camphor flakes. No longer doing this, we all wondered, where did the moths go?

As I imagined the strong smell of camphor, my mind was transported back in time to my childhood home. An apartment on Graham Avenue in Brooklyn that was above a furniture and lighting store, my age, no more than three. I woke up from a nap and heard my uncle and mother talking in the kitchen. Sitting up in my crib, the smell of camphor surrounded me. I noticed a small red wool bag filled with a harsh smell around my neck. On my hands were my socks. My face felt hot and itchy and my arms were covered with red polka dots. I cried, all I wanted to do was *rattari, rattari* (scratch, scratch.) My mother came in and explained, "The camphor will make all the spots come out, the red bag was to ward off evil, and the socks will stop your nails from taking off the scabs that will otherwise leave scars. Measles are catching and I'm hoping your brother will get them too. Now there would be one less childhood disease to worry about."

Growing up we were soon introduced to more folk remedies. The smelliest was mustard plaster. Half a teaspoon of mustard-seed powder was mixed with a tablespoon of flour adding just enough water to make a paste. Sandwiched between two pieces of flannel cloth, it was applied to your chest for the discomfort of colds and congestion. Arthritis and muscle aches were also treated this way. Careful, could cause burning of the skin, check every five minutes and remove as soon as discomfort happens. It remained in place no longer than fifteen minutes.

A recipe for a drink to soothe coughs was, first put a teaspoon in a glass so it will not break from the heat. Then, a few squeezes of lemon juice, a clove of mashed garlic and fill with strong brewed tea, a spoonful of honey and two teaspoons of whiskey. It may not cure you, but you don't care as much. Soon sleepy time would take over ZZZ's...

Winter time found my brother Frank's head under a towel while his face was over a basin filled with one tablespoon of Vicks VapoRub and four cups of hot water, great for relief of a head cold.

Without too much leaping and jumping I would allow my mother to apply a little Vicks on my chest and a dab in my nostrils. This was enough to help me breathe. I have always been a believer of, "*comu veni, si nni va*" (the way it comes is the way it goes.)

Boiled water and fennel seeds strained and cooled were used for a baby with colic and adults with a stomach ache.

An onion cut in half and rubbed on a bee sting brought relief from itch.

If cut while in the woods, gathered spider webs on a stick were placed on the cut to stop the bleeding.

A small cross made with thumbnail on a mosquito bite and a little spit or salt applied would stop the itch.

Chewing mint leaves relieved garlic breath.

A hot potato placed in a sock and applied to your ear soon brought relief from an earache.

For itchy feet, oil covered garlic cloves allowed to soak a few days then strained, placing just the oil on your itching burning feet for relief.

For corns on your feet, apply a stale piece of bread soaked in vinegar and secure overnight. Morning brings amazing results.

For teething infants, rub whiskey directly on the gums. For older children and adults, sip whiskey, but do not swallow. Hold liquid in your mouth on the side that is painful, and it will numb the pain.

Breastfeeding mothers were told to drink beer with dinner as the hops would be beneficial to their babies. This was also beneficial for the mothers as this, at times, put the baby to sleep.

These were day-to-day folk remedies with no scientific proof and no side effects.

Mamma's kitchen was the hub of our families' wheel. This was the day my eyes could not believe what I was seeing. My family, that I knew I loved and trusted and were powerful against all evil, today stood silent around my father whose back was exposed. The nameless, faceless man was applying small glasses (shot glasses) filled with smoke. A small piece of cotton set on fire was placed inside the glass and quickly extinguished to starve the oxygen. This was applied to his back, which lifted the skin into a welt inside the glass. It was explained to me that this would bring blood to the congested area and bring relief to the lungs. In the end, my father's back looked like a mythical animal skin with rows of ragin circles. This was called Cupping.

Many remedies have been introduced into my life. Cupping is the most vivid, violent, and disturbing of all.

A Fairytale Life

Many times, I was told I lived a fairytale life. Neighbors, friends, and relatives would often say, "The way you live is very special." They were right. Frank and I were blessed to be surrounded with unconditional love. With a mother, father, grandmother, two aunts, and two uncles, that treated us like a prince and a princess. We were often told if there was something we truly wanted, we had only to ask. Strangely, the more we were offered, the less important monetary things became.

We went fishing, we learned to plant and harvest fruits and vegetables. Sundays were kept special with family and friends. We attended The Academy of Music on Saturdays to experience the world of opera; Pagliacci the clown and Carmen the gypsy were my favorite. A Sunday walk in Highland Park which ended with a box of Crackerjacks or a hot pastrami sandwich on a cold winter's night was an enjoyable experience. At night we listened to "My Friend Irma" on the radio, watched The "Ed Sullivan Show" or Elvis for the first time on TV. This is the life that people saw. But as my mother would say, "Only the spoon knows the pot it stirs." *Sulu a cucchiara sapi la pignata ca rimina.* But, as in every fairytale, there are always two sides to a story.

My mother suffered with severe headaches; she often said that a sorcerer must have put a spell on her. She traveled far and wide to find a bespeckled white coated elder that could take this spell away. "Arthritis" they said, "was an evil curse with no remedy." "Keep a song in your heart and a smile on your lips, and try to enjoy life," she was told. At times I found her with a bandana around her forehead which contained sliced potatoes. "Why?" I asked, she replied that she was told by a wizened old woman that their juice had curative powers. My mother did not know why it made her feel better. Was it the coolness, or was it, in fact, the juice of the potatoes? She confided that to rid herself of this headache, she would eat anything, drink anything, or even try those needles that the Chinese believed in.

My father was enchanted by the way my mother could stretch the money he earned, making him feel proud in front of friends and family. He often remarked, "She keeps a beautiful home, saves enough money to buy a new car, and we eat well every night." At home, my mother was always well dressed, ready for uninvited guests.

And then enlightenment came. On a freezing day in the winter of 1947, the boiler in school burst, and we were sent home early. Opening the door, I saw my mother wearing my father's wool pants and flannel shirt. All I could say was, "Mom, why?" "Ah," she said, "Now I will tell you my secret, so that when you become the queen of your castle you will know the sacrifices it takes to make everything appear wonderful. You see, as soon as you and your brother leave for school, I shut off the heat while I clean the house. It gets so cold that your father's wool pants and flannel shirt keep me warm. The longer the kerosene lasts the more money I save. When you were surprised to see me eat leftover meat on a Friday, it meant that there would be more fish for the rest of you. Changing buttons and trim on my dress, gives me the money to buy you a new one. Now remember, this is our secret. We are the spoon (*cucchiara*) and our castle is our pot (*pignata*)."

My parents shared their wisdom, and taught us through their Sicilian proverbs. My father's favorite proverb was, "*Fa beni e scordatillu, fa mali e ricordatillu*" "Do good things and forget — do evil and remember it". He felt blessed he said as long as he could help others, God blessed him because he didn't need help. Good deeds are to be kept quiet. It's between God and you.

As astrology tells us, a Sagittarius man possesses the intensity of the inner core of a flame. He worked with iron that was manipulated and bent to his will with a hammer and his sheer force. Amazed was he when *Lu malu lupu*, the evil wolf, came out of the shadows, gripped his heart and bent it to his will. *Lu malu lupu* was always lurking and they fought a tug-o-war of life and death for many years.

I fell ill with pneumonia, which in the 1940's was serious enough to warrant hospitalization. The wise bespeckled white coated elder said there was a new potion, but only if my mother gave written permission could it be administered. She signed and agreed and penicillin entered my body. Soon I was well.

Frank, stood on what he thought was earth as hard as a crocodile's spine. As he reached over a barbed wire fence, he slid down on a slimy toad and impaled himself by his armpit. The kite he tried to reach remained on the other side. Back and forth to the far away island of Manhattan he and my mother traveled. The doctor they met had great knowledge of veins and muscles, and helped Frank to heal.

Time passed quickly, as adults we still had and enjoyed our loved ones. Now, our babies flourished in the warmth of their smiles and good nature.

And then on the eve of Memorial Day 1970, my father followed his heart, always vigilant of other's needs. He told my mother, "Cook the pasta, I won't be long." He went across the street to be sure that my aunt Annie and uncle Lorenzo had enough medicine since tomorrow, Memorial Day; all the stores would be closed. As he was returning home, he turned the doorknob, opened the door and *Lu malu lupu* waited for him on the other side. He gripped and stilled my father's ailing heart. The angel of death swept in, encircling him with black feathery wings.

My father's only life's request of the exulted one of the higher realm was, keep my mind sane for three days after death, to know where I've been, where I am, and where I am going. Several years later, on October 19th which would have been their wedding anniversary, my mother and father were reunited.

And so, they will continue to live "Happily ever after" in our heart and memories.

City Girl - Country Girl

Here I stand with broken shoes, dusty socks, and pants ripped at the knee. The ever present band-aid peeking through my pink and white striped seersucker pedal pusher pants with stains of Mercurochrome red. That meant the fall from the tree was not so bad. If Mamma, my grandmother said in broken English, "getta da iodine," watch out. You knew that the cut was bad. She would apply the dark red burning stuff from the bottle with the rubber stopper. As she washed out the gravel, plucked at the splinters, or removed the thorns, you knew that you would screech like a cat whose tail got caught under a rocking chair.

As she applied the iodine, she would say, "*sciuscia, sciuscia, comu lu ventu*" blow, blow like the wind. Her distraction made the pain and suffering less. Torture over, iodine stopper replaced, her kiss on my head, and with the screen door banging, I was back at play.

Living in the country for the months of July and August was liberation. Starched clothes, ruffled lace socks, school days, homework and early bedtime were forgotten. On the last day of school we would twirl and sing, "No more pencils, no more books, no more teachers' dirty looks."

16

Today was Wednesday the date, middle of August, 1943. The Rosedale country kids called my brother and me "the summer kids." Everyone was running and yelling, the ice man is coming, the ice man is coming. The old ice truck bounced in and out of potholes and stopped at our door. We knew he would lift the dirty burlap sacks covering the large blocks of ice. As we surrounded his truck he would use his ice pick to chip the ice this way and that way, allowing us to enjoy the spray of ice crystals.

The best was yet to come. As he disappeared into the house, the boys, Frank, Pete, Louie, and Frankie, would jump on the back of the rickety old truck, chipping large pieces of ice, throwing them onto the dirt. We all ran to find this frozen treasure that not only cleaned itself, but refreshed our parched skin. As it ran down our necks, it gave us a shiver. In Sicilian when you fidgeted, the elders would say *"Chi fa, pisci e tremi?"* or as we called it, "The Pee-Pee Dance." The returning ice man would cause us to scatter with the treasure of the day, ICE; COLD, WET ICE. . .

Dolly

As we decorated the house for my birthday party, Mommy and I were chatting about how grown-up I would be. We talked about getting a big bed so that I could have sleepovers, walking the dog, and going to first grade. We both knew that buying a new doll for my birthday was the best thing. Shirley Temple was a seven year-old, real live girl that was called a child star. She sang and danced in the movies to the song "The Good Ship Lollypop." Everyone loved her bouncy, blonde curls. All my school friends wanted a tall, girl-sized Shirley Temple doll and so did I.

The next day, off we went to Mr. Jay's toy store on Broadway in Brooklyn. Entering the store, my eyes looked this way and that way. I had never seen so many different dolls. Red-heads, blondes, brunettes, baby dolls in diapers and some with real fur coats and ice skates. Looking at my blonde curls, the toy man smiled and said, "Straight ahead for Shirley dolls." All the tall boxes stood around the cash register. In each was a stiff doll that looked like a fairy-tale child frozen by a wicked witch. Shaking my head I said, "Oh no, no! I don't want her!" Round and round I went looking for a dolly that was soft, lovable, and huggable. There she was with brownish-blonde curls, eyes that opened and closed with real eyelashes, and pretty pink lips with a little hole to hold a bottle. To my surprise, when Mr. Jay put her in my arms, she said "Ma-ma." I hugged her and felt she was already mine.

That night, the whole family tried to find a perfect name. Susie, Veronica, Ellie, Jane? No, no, no and no. My father, with a quizzical look, said, "Cecelia, you treat your dolly like a queen, and in Italian *Regina* means queen." Yes, that was a perfect name. My mother was already crocheting her a blanket that looked like a million scallop shells on a pink, sandy beach. She used my two pointer fingers and, wrapping ribbon around them, she tied perfect little bows that sat on the blanket.

The next day, with *Regina* in her carriage, I played outside. Amanda, a new girl on the block, came over to play. She looked into my doll carriage and said with her nose in the air, "What kind of doll is THAT?" Excitedly, I told her it was a baby doll and that it says "Ma-ma." Her nose wrinkled and her lips were pursed like a pig's puss. Sounding like an old goat she cleared her throat and said, "Oh, well I have a Shirley doll." Shirley was sitting in her carriage and looked like a stiff swordfish (*piscispata*) with a baby bonnet on – how silly! I giggled and she walked away quickly, still with her pig puss on (*vucca di porcu*).

Quickly, picking *Regina* up, I ran to my mother. As I was telling her what had happened, she smiled and said, "You're like her real mother. You loved dolly when you saw her, you chose to call her *Regina*, and she called you "Ma-Ma." "Look how offended you are at what Amanda said. Twist and turn, Amanda's doll will always be, just Shirley." Tightly, I hugged *Regina* and knew that all the Shirley Dolls in the world couldn't change the love I felt for my Dolly.

Just Rags

"Ten cents!"

"Five cents!"

The bickering went on and on. Time passed as I watched the men with their black vests, white shirts, black pants with prayer strings at their waists, and yarmulkes on their heads with odd curls showing. The women wore long skirts and kerchiefs while pulling along their little children. There were a lot of differences here.

Soon, out of the doorway came my grandmother. "*Veni, camina* (come, walk)," she said. "He has junk." As I started to get up, Mr. Jacob, the Jewish merchant, appeared. Shaking his head, the words were always the same. "Lady, lady, come back! I'll show you quality."

My grandmother would continue:

"Don't give me a burnt piece!"

"Make sure the line is straight!"

"Are you sure that's the best price you can give me?"

Finally, they settled on seven cents. Her purchases of rags and trims were wrapped in brown paper, tied with string and put into a shopping bag. This was called *la strada degli ebrei* (the street of the Jews).

The Jews came to America to avoid persecution in Eastern Europe. Many continued to be merchants. Here they lived, worked, and carved new lives in the tenements. This was the ultimate flea market. Push carts, fruit stands, and even the poor, worn-out horses wore pots and pans attached to their bridles. Communication was done through grunts, broken English and hand gestures. Money was the universal language – everyone understood it. Mamma held my hand tight. She was afraid I'd get lost, or that the Gypsies would take me and sell me. Blonde-haired little girls were special – they were sold for gold coins.

Never would I be able to find this place on my own. She quickly ran down an alley, between two buildings and up a few water-soaked steps to the center of the tenements' courtyards. The merchants lived in hovels filled with underwear, shoes, and loose buttons. There was nothing you couldn't find here – you simply needed to ask, or use your hands, to describe it. The smell of burnt, water-soaked fabric is still vivid in my mind. Lace and trim would find themselves on the edges of sheets and pillowcases. Holiday tablecloths were surrounded by the best of lace. Even my simple cotton slips were adorned. That day, we left with two yards of rags – one black with little yellow flowers and one blue with pink stripes. These were neatly folded and put away.

The end of June soon came; school was over and we packed up to stay with my grandmother for two months. We knew from the past that the first rainy day would bring out the rags. Each piece of rag was laid on the table – a makeshift pattern made from newspaper was prepared. The pattern consisted of the main part – the waistband, two deep pockets, and two long strings. Mamma cut and Frank pinned the pieces together. When he pricked his finger he would mutter boy words – bad boy words. Mamma would smile and say, "don't get blood on my new aprons!" Needle in hand, I basted with long stitches under her watchful eye before she completed them on the sewing machine. No longer a rag, it became a cover over our shivering shoulders when we came out of the sprinklers. Lifting the two corners, it was a carrier for the vegetables, grapes, and figs. As my brother chased me, I would hide under the apron and know that I was safe and invisible. Teaching us the *tarantella* while lifting her apron as if it were a ball gown, Mamma danced and sang with us. Best of all, she took off the apron and, using the strings, made whipping sounds. We would gallop like horses with Mamma in close pursuit.

As years passed, the horses I imagined always changed. First it was Pegasus, a white horse with large wings that magically flew. Once I was older, I imagined the black stallion Toronado, as ridden by Zorro, the popular movie hero. I would follow Frank on his white stallion while I carried a whip made from a slender branch. The year came when Frank decided he was too grown to continue playing these childish games. As time went on, I noticed my grandmother stopped more often to pretend we were watering the horses.

Soon, summer was over. This would be the last time we would fly in a make-believe world. Mamma went back to her apartment and we went back to our house. When we visited her, not a hair was out of place. She wore a starched, stiff, store-bought apron and sat as the family's matriarch. Her persona in the city changed – no one suspected that she ran barefoot around the house like a little child. The twinkle in her blue eyes and warm smile remained. As she hugged us she said, "*vola, cavaddu!* (fly, horse!)"

Who knew that a rag – plus love – could become a magical, royal cloth?

Jewish Market Place Watercolor By Cecelia.

A Tale of Two Tails

Glenmore 5, Applegate 7 and Evergreen 6, were all Brooklyn telephone exchanges in the early 1950's.

Our elders were resistant to anything new. With a wave of both hands as though to dismiss the thought of a telephone, my grandmother said, "Why do I need one?" "Who's going to call me?" Where do I put it?" But enticed by the new daily gossip of who called who, she soon agreed.

The ladies found that a half round table with a crocheted doily was the perfect place. The phone numbers were placed neatly on the side, just in case of an emergency.

Hearing our new telephone ring was exciting. Who could be calling us? Standing still I heard my mother say, "Hello, hello," as she motioned with her hand and a shrug of her shoulders. "Who is it?" "Who is it?" "Oh, Mama." Distancing the receiver from her ear, we heard my grandmother say, "AHHHH, AHHHH." "Jennie, my dear daughter-in-law, I'm ready and dressed for the *manicomiu,* insane asylum." Listening, we heard her tell about the sausage. It was a circle tied special link by link with white butcher string by Tony the butcher. He delivered it that afternoon and now it was gone.

For dinner she was making pasta with beans and fried sausage (*pasta câ fasola e sasizza fritta*). She left the sausage on the table. Three rings of the doorbell was her signal that the postman had a letter from Sicily. Quickly she ran to the door and returning with the letters in hand, she saw the sausage was gone. Only the white butcher paper was there.

She has been looking and looking all afternoon. First she looked in the refrigerator, then the stove, cupboards and the washing machine, even under the bed. She was now convinced that the spirits had taken the sausage. As she spoke, her voice became calm. "Now I will rethink dinner, but tomorrow first thing, Jennie, please come and help me find the sausage." "Of course," my mother said.

Hearing about his mother's tale of woe, my father smiled and said, "Did she look in the mailbox?" Quickly my mother dialed the number and delivered the message. We could hear the clickety-clack of her shoes running down the hallway. Returning, out of breath she said, "NO."

The next morning at 7:30, once again my grandmother called. Laughing uncontrollably she said, "Jennie, don't hurry over I found the sausage. I got up early because the dog was barking and barking and chasing his tail around and around. As he walked away, I saw two tails, his curly tail and the white butcher string trailing behind."

"Now the sausage is gone and nature will take care of the string. I guess the men in the white coats will wait for another day."

A Fathers' Blind Rage

Like a hawk grabbing its prey, my mother held my hand. It seemed like a procession of women, men, and children going down Meserole Street. Tony the butcher, it was said, had committed the unthinkable. The chattering continued until we were in front of the butcher shop on Scholes Street. Gasps, signs of the cross, and "*Madonna mia*" were heard up and down the street. Facing the large butcher shop window, I saw the long, sharp, pointy, three-pronged metal hook that usually held rabbits at Christmas time. Today it was holding a bloody piece of meat. The women, some blushing, some pointing, others moving in closer to make sure they were correct in what they were looking at, were all in a state of shock, while other women took turns telling what they had heard. They continued. He trusted someone he didn't know? How could a mother leave an innocent child with a stranger? What would possess a grown man to take advantage of his benefactors' twelve year old daughter?

Tony, the butcher, had opened his home to this discouraged man with no trade and no future, and taught him to be a butcher. He would brag and say, "This is the brother I never had. I would trust him with my life and my money."

Tony and his wife had left to attend an afternoon wedding. In that short time, the man had his way with the young daughter, reducing her to a walking zombie. Returning home, Tony found her with eyes red from crying and her dress torn.

Tony found the scoundrel hiding in his yard and with his knife cut the man as if he was back in Sicily working with his father in the art of gelding horses and mules. This was done to the animals to remove their desire to mate. This act, being performed on a human, caused the man to die.

The police took the dead man away and Tony to jail. Weeks passed and we heard Tony's wife, whose heart was filled with tears, had moved away and that the young girl was sent to live with the nuns at the convent.

Rumors continued…

A Matter of Heart

The butcher was on the phone. "Jennie, come quick, your mother needs you." He continued that there had been a misunderstanding in his shop, and Mamma had to be helped upstairs. Our German neighbor was kind enough to drive us. Arriving, we were approached by a gathering of neighbors ready to explain what went on. They all began to talk at once. A wave of my mother's hand and we rushed up the stairs. The apartment door was opened and we stepped into a kitchen that resembled my brother's pigeon coop at feeding time. Neighbors were drinking coffee, bobbing their heads and pecking into the familiar white cookie box which had contained Sunday's cookies. Someone I didn't recognize was looking into "*lu casciuni,*" the familiar large junk drawer. This is where my grandmother kept her gas and electric bills. Along the side, the extra money for the insurance man and the man that brought a gallon of javel water, bleach, each week. If you asked for a lost toy, a skate key, Frank's rubber band ball, or the block of tin foil collected from the cigarette packs, Mamma would point to the drawer. It was upsetting to me; privacy was respected in our family.

Going into Mamma's bedroom, my eyes were wide with what I saw. She looked like a mannequin with a flushed face and a wet cloth, not on her forehead, but on top of her head. She told my mother she felt as if she had "*u corpu di sangu*", which translated into "a body of blood". This could cause a stroke or paralysis. What astonished me the most was that she had her outdoor shoes on her bedspread. It was Saturday and so the bed was dressed and ready for company, with a blue silky quilted bedspread. We were taught that a bed was to be made first thing in the morning and was for sleeping only. From the kitchen we heard my Uncle Jimmy thanking the neighbors and wishing them a good evening as he locked the door behind them.

Seeing her children there, my grandmother began recounting the events of the afternoon. "Luigi," she said, had been despondent; his mother was constantly criticizing him. And so Mamma's motherly heart hurt for him. He now had an opportunity to make money but he needed five hundred dollars to buy into an established beauty salon. No one believed in him. A loan for a month or two was all he needed. My grandmother's soft heart won over her good sense. She said she would help him, and so six months ago she told him to come up with his mother and she would have his money. The day came and he came alone, dressed in his suit with frayed cuffs and a diamond horseshoe stick pin that was upside down in his tie. She continued, for the moment I thought, no wonder his luck has run out. As she slid the money across the table in an envelope, his composure changed. She became skeptical of the several excuses he made for his misfortune. Tossing the envelope, he put the money into his breast pocket. She again told him that she had been saving the money to bring forth her lifetime dream of becoming a land owner. It was common in Sicily when her parents died, the land they owned was given only to the sons. She was promised to be married to a man much older than her. She had no choice but to marry this man with a son that was 18 years old. When out shopping and asked if he was her brother, with cast down eyes she answered "No, he is my son." Her brothers thought the older man would be able to support her. Instead, after they had four additional children, he left to make his fortune in America. She remained in Sicily to raise her family alone. Many years passed and he sent word for her to come to America. As life would have it, she soon became a widow. Here in America, after many, many years of saving, she was told by the real estate man in Rosedale, Queens that a plot of land attached to their summer home would soon become available. Uncle Jimmy and Aunt Lena supported her and she had saved every penny possible. This was to be a surprise for her children. She was amazed that as an uneducated woman, she could actually purchase land. This would be her American dream.

Where to begin? This afternoon, she went to the butcher shop and chose the meat she wanted for dinner. As she went to pay for it, the butcher, in a low voice said, "Not to worry, Donna Rosina," as he licked the point of his pencil and began to write in his ledger. "You can pay me later." I asked him, "Why do you think I cannot pay cash?" "Well," he said, "Luigi and his mother told everyone that your family has fallen on hard times and that you have been harassing Luigi for the few dollars that you lent to him." As I looked around, the customers were whispering to each other. This was the first time that she felt that she had made "a *mala figura*" presented a bad image and brought shame and embarrassment to herself and her hard working children. As she began to leave, she saw the two culprits run down into the subway station. This caused her knees to tremble and her anger to escalate.

My uncle bent down and said to her what we had heard her say so often, "*Mamma, cosi ca succedunu e vivi, a li morti 'un ci succedi nenti.*" "These are things that happen to the living, nothing happens anymore to the dead." Looking at both ladies, he said, "Tomorrow, Luigi will bring a white envelope. Mamma, this is not a social call, it is just for him to return what belongs to you. He will ask for your forgiveness. It is up to you, forgive him or not. It is not necessary to count the money; all you receive belongs to you."

The following day we asked Mamma, "Did you forgive him?" Her only response was, "*Tra amici e parenti 'un accatari e vinniri nenti.*" "Between friends and family, don't buy or sell anything." Her decision remains a mystery...

Williamsburg Watercolor By Cecelia

Nature's Call

The little grey structure was made with a peaked roof, louvered window and front door with a half moon. In front, my mother had planted some *sciuri di* notti (night-blooming flowers) and added a window box.

"Quick, hurry – I've got to go!" *In campagna*, this was the only bathroom (*stanza di bagnu*) we had.

Inside, the usual hole down to never-never-land was surrounded by a toilet seat. It sat on a bench with carved corbels and grooved columns — fancy enough to be in the house. Uncle Jimmy, or Zizi as we called him, was a fine cabinet maker. He built a shelf which held a dark blue lantern, a box for matches, and even a place for magazines and comic books. Always present was a toilet paper caddy – a doll with a crocheted skirt that, when lifted, exposed the next colored toilet paper roll. Pink, yellow, or my favorite, blue.

At night, we would notice the work the spiders did with the eight spinnerets located on their bellies. Large webs were anchored so that the vibrations would be felt when a moth or a fly was trapped. The shadows cast by the lantern light were interesting; we too made shadows with bent fingers, creating dogs and butterflies.

When you were inside, you always knew who had cleaned that day. My mother used bath salts with rose petals and a vase filled with lavender branches; no-nonsense mamma combined branches of oregano, mint, and basil to freshen the aroma. Even still, at times it was necessary to raise your eyebrows, lower your eyelids and wrinkle your nose to complete nature's call. It was a place we didn't want to go, but always did.

My father told us a funny story that we could repeat to our city friends when they were hesitant about using the outhouse. When he first came to America, he joined his family on George Street in Brooklyn. Venturing to the outhouse, he was surprised by what was used as toilet paper – magazines, newspaper pages, and Sears and Roebuck catalog advertisements. Sometimes, they were treated to the papers which surrounded fruit for shipping and protection. These were held to the wall with a nail. One day, everyone he met from the building went to lean against the wall and scratch their behinds. Some of the ladies were genteel about this; some of the older men openly scratched. Could it have been their *mutanni di lana* (woolen underwear)? No – it was the middle of summer. The culprit, they found, were the papers which surrounded the *ficud'india* (prickly pears). These harbor tiny splinters that go undetected, until they get under your skin.

Careful what you use!

The Outhouse Watercolor By Cecelia

More Than a Friendly Visit

The bus was taking us to a friend of my mother's. Asking, "Mom, who is she," she began, "she is the daughter of my *cummari* who is married to the son of your father's *cumpari*." As children, we were taught to be cordial, kiss everyone that came to visit and call them aunt or uncle. "Please, Mom, stop!" I said. I had lost my way with the whole family tree, "just tell me when to ring the bell so we can get off the bus." There were times when you arrived late at a family gathering and had to kiss everyone hello that was sitting around the table. It took awhile for me to understand that these were not all my relatives.

Finally, it was time to ring the bell, ding, ding. We got off the bus, with an overflowing shopping bag and cookie box in hand; I noticed that we were not far from Mamma's home. I had never been to this complex which was several stories high. Many returning soldiers and their families resided here. This was called the Projects on Bushwick Avenue and Scholes Street. The grounds were designed to look park-like, built where old tenements had been. We entered the large marble foyer, filled with tenants getting their mail and waiting for the elevator. We took the elevator to the top floor. The hallway was filled with children running back and forth, it resembled a goat farm with boys bumping heads, tumbling, and yelling. We asked if they knew where Maria lived, two of the boys led the way. My mother knocked and entered the hallway calling out to Maria. A gruff male voice responded harshly from the front room, "who is it?" "Peter, it's Jennie," my mother answered, dead silence. My mother looked at me and said, "*menzu cretinu*", this always made me laugh, it translated into a piece of idiot. Asking my mother why she called him that, she responded that Maria's husband was not even smart enough to be a whole idiot.

The dining room looked like it threw up. Old food and new food on the table, a little boy with no diaper cried as his siblings taunted him for urinating on the floor. My mother called out again, "Hello, Maria?" "Here" she said, "in the kitchen." She was sitting in front of the stove, a pot of boiling diapers smelled of ammonia. Maria had one baby suckling at her breast while she rocked another in a cradle with her foot. In the corner was the usual carton filled with home-work. These were pieces of clothing that needed to be finished by hand. The women sewed buttons, beads or cuffs. Giving Maria the box of pastries and the shopping bag, she lifted her head. The color surrounding her eye was black, blue and purple, resembling an eggplant. My mother was taken aback. Maria said "Please, take back the sweets; I would rather have the money for Peter." Her sons had opened the box leaving only the cardboard box, string and a few crumbs. My mother gave her some money and tried to be diplomatic and tolerant, asking, "What happened." Maria said it was her fault because she didn't keep the house clean and did not look pretty anymore. She said she reached "*na strata senza uscita*," a dead end street. If I had my brother's catcher's mitt I could have caught my mother's raised eyebrow hearing her friend take all the blame. My mother did a few chores and we left on Marias' insistence. She appreciated the help, but Peter would not.

That night at home, my mother was preparing dinner, fried fish, pasta with cauliflower (*cavulisciuri*), and toasted breadcrumbs as a topping which was called poor man's cheese. It was also called St. Joseph's sawdust since he was a carpenter and also the earthly father to Jesus. We, the family, continued dressing our salad. Holding the heavy bottomed glistening aluminum frying pan with the pox marks in her hand and twirling it to distribute the oil she said, "I am going to call this frying pan Maria and give it to her. The next time, she may want to introduce it to Peter and give him a little ping to wake him up." I wondered if Peter would ever see the frying pan, or would it be stored out of sight?

You see, my mother explained the reason for our visit today; it was to see how Maria was and to show me another side of life. Maria's own mother could not go, she too was in an abusive marriage with little money and no room in her home. Not wanting to show favoritism for her daughter or go against her son-in-law, she told her daughter to "raise your children and make the best of it."

Spousal abuse was spoken about in hushed voices behind drawn shades and closed doors. Both men and women did not want anyone to know what went on inside their home. Men were subjected to abuse by their bosses while working on the railroad or the slaughter houses in Greenpoint. Some were on the docks at the Brooklyn Navy Yard. At home they drank excessively and took their frustration out on wives and children. Young women often times were sent from their home in Sicily and promised a better life only to find hardship and isolation here in America. They would retaliate by abusing their husbands and children. They fought an internal conflict daily.

Abuse has no heart, crosses the boundaries of the rich, poor, young and old and leaves boot-prints on your heart. Still they were reminded that the Sicilian proverb "*Cu lassa la vecchia pi la nova sapi chiddu chi lassa - ma nun sapi chiddu ca trova*" translated; who leaves the old for the new knows what they have, but does not know what they will find. Many were convinced that this was true more times than not. . .

Just His Way

Everyone was sleeping. My aunt Annie and I were in the middle of the road. Looking this way and that, we saw not a soul in sight. Only the bats were circling the street lamp. The houses were all dark and the woods that I played in were lit with fireflies. Shadows of tree limbs through the streetlights clawed at the road. Here *in campagna*, (country) almost midnight, and still he was not home. The crickets and cicadas were singing loudly, both looking for a mate and letting the world know that tomorrow would be a scorching, hot day. A mosquito buzzed in my ear, landed on my arm and with a quick ping, he was no more. Quickly we returned to the basement and waited. We finished playing cards, and coloring in my book. We even played *"Issa gatta,"* you put one hand down, the other person covered your hand and this continued. Then you would quickly pull one hand out and then the other, soon it looked like a cat was trying to catch a mouse. As we sat and waited, sleep was winning out. My eyes were starting to spin. To keep me awake, my aunt began, "I'm going to tell you a story. Back in Sicily, Donna Maria had a husband who had the same characteristics as our own gadabout (habitual fun seeker). He was the life of every one's party, but when he came home he was tired and grumpy. Even if by accident, you bumped his foot, he would open one eye and growl at you. Donna Maria often lamented that her husband was, *"spassu dî vicini e trivolu di casa."* That was her story.

This is our story. Today I was my aunt's interpreter. We had to go in front of the judge. A few days ago, our gadabout was taken away and put behind bars. Forgetting about her accent, my aunt pleaded with the judge. "Please, your honor, he is good and very friendly, he was provoked. No, he never did that before." The judge looked at me and said, "She loves him very much, and I will let him go home." We said, "Thank you, Your Honor," and left. When we got home, a neighbor-lady with a snide look and crooked smile said, "Anna, I would have kicked him to the curb or tied him to a tree; you are too good to him." My aunt couldn't resist as she said to me, *"Lu immurutu menza a via lu su immu 'un sû talia"* (the hunchback never sees his own hump). The busybody had a house full of problems, but like the hunchback she never saw her own, only everyone else's.

As the clock bonged twelve, we looked up and saw his legs impatiently passing back and forth across the basement windows. My

34

aunt went up to let him in. In a stern voice she said, "You smell terrible, you were at the stable again." As she placed a bowl of water on the floor, Skippy jumped up and kissed her. Wagging his tail he waited to be petted, "Yes, yes," she said, "I love you, but you are a bad, bad dog."

And now he is home, she is happy, and I can finally go to sleep.

Cecelia, Frankie, Frank and Skippy.

Holy Week Brings New Beginnings

When you prepare for Palm Sunday and Easter week, the house gets cleaned from stove top to basement windows. Lace curtains were washed, starched and stretched on a wooden frame. They had pins so sharp that a few piercings were to be expected. Ceilings were washed, rooms were painted and rugs were taken outside and beaten with an old broom.

So many years have passed, but memories never dim. As I prepared for Easter 2011, I reminisced about the 1950's. During Easter season, going to church was a time of sadness, reflection, and finally joy. Seeing the statues covered with a purple veil reminded us to reflect on the Passion of Christ and not be distracted by the images. Our focus was on the events that led up to the resurrection. It is told that the color purple was used by the rich to show their power and royalty. The finest purple color came from a spiny shellfish known as a Murex mollusk. A purple robe and a crown of thorns were used to mock Jesus as a king prior to being crucified. I was mesmerized by the piercings of the thorns that encircled the head of Jesus, and how he suffered for us.

After my confirmation I was at an age when as I sat in the church, all our teachings came alive. I can still visualize to the right side the Nativity, this baby born unto us. Facing the front, over the altar you see Jesus on the cross. To the left of the altar, there was a Pietà, Mother Mary holding her dead son in her arms. The smell of hand lit candles and incense increased our joy for the resurrection. Sicilians do not suppress emotions when it comes to religion. We are encouraged to realize the pain when we pierced ourselves on the thorns of a rose bush. We are taught to remember God. Joy was described as a happy heart. Listening to Bible stories helped us form our moral fibers. As a child we were afraid to sin and displease God. As an adult, church told us to do things for the love of God. Christian legend says that carnations appeared when a tear of Mother Mary fell to the ground at her son's crucifixion. Carnations represent a Mother's undying love. On Mother's Day, the men wore a red carnation if Mother was alive and a white carnation if Mother was dead. As children we looked for the white carnations, trying to imagine how their mother died. Women wore pink.

On Palm Sunday we brought our palms to Mr. Joe across from Mamma's. He was an old craftsman who still enjoyed working with his hands. The palm fronds were turned into braided crosses. each a work of art that we tucked under the mattress. His unmarried sisters, who we called *"li signurini"* were expert bakers. The smell of vanilla, almond paste and cinnamon filled the hallway. Our visit on Easter Sunday was always a treat. They waited for us to pick out the colored eggs which they then baked in bread shaped like a dove. The two sisters and their brother beamed with sincere geniality and were most generous. Frank and I sang along with them.

Un cappidduzzu
Ah truvavi un cappidduzzu, bedd'e sapuritu,
Quannu mi l'ai a mettiri?
Quannu mi fazzu zitu,

This was a childhood song about a boy who found a little hat and how he would wear it when he married. Conversation for the men was about *primavera* the beautiful season, the rotation of planting and the distribution of seeds from Sicily. Mr. Joe was called upon to prune or graft the grape arbors. Two buds on the new wood were necessary for success. Gently he cut a V-shape in one branch and then fitted it to another and wrapped it with cloth that had been soaked in his elixir. This helped the final joining of white and purple grapes, enticing them to grow on one stem. Their kitchen corner was filled with cast-offs, chairs, pots, pans and all things that would soon travel to their country home in Elmont.

Sicilians love *"un pezzu di terra e la casuzza di campagna"* a piece of earth and a country home. If you are Sicilian, you know that some summer homes were in fact a garage. First the garage was built, the big house was built later, if ever. The entire garage space is divided into a big bedroom and a little bedroom, no living room was needed. The indoor kitchen table was used for all waking hours if it was raining or if the mosquitoes were feasting on you. The outdoor table under the arbor was for entertaining, long winded discussions and wine tasting. The outhouse was in the back of the lot. The farm resembled a labyrinth and took up the remaining space. Women took care of herbs and flowers, while men would dig with a pitch fork or a large hoe or sledge hammer. My father called it *"Lu Mazzu."* Sicilian proverb describing a family was *"tanti testi-tanti mazzi."* Many heads –many hammers. Visualize the family in a circle, each trying to strike the same spot. Simply translated, a family has many individual ideas that they bring together, each wants to be heard and have his idea implemented.

Buona Pasqua e Primavera - To live simple was a blessing.

Proud Sicilian - American,
my Grandfather.

Donna Filomina

At 224 Bushwick Avenue in Brooklyn, the outside door opened only after you rang the bell and waited for a buzz back. As you entered, your sense of smell was assaulted by fried fish, chicken soup, roasted peppers or pungent broccoli. This tenement had six families with the owners' butcher shop on the ground floor.

Tenement living was made up of private apartments with front doors usually left open. Neighbors and their visiting relatives walked in and out unannounced. This was where my grandmother, Mamma, my mothers' family lived since coming to America. Mamma lived on the second floor, but, scary Donna Filomina lived on the first floor . . .

Donna Filomina was an ancient women with wispy, grey hair combed into a *tuppu*, a bun, on the top of her head. Her eyes were black, I think. You see, I never really looked into them for fear of *lu Mal'uocchiu,* the evil eye. She wore an apron with big pockets that held herbs for stomach aches and oils for muscle strains. Her shawl was black with fringe and she smelled of cats. She always mumbled, or was she praying or perhaps rehashing an incantation gone wrong.

My brother Frank would always find a way to push me into her back door which you had to pass to get upstairs. Then he would raise his arms; wiggle his fingers and whisper, "whooo whooo she's going to cook you". Scared I said, "Mom, he's saying it again". To Frank she said "*finiscila!*" end it. To give me a sense of power over fear, my mother said "put your fingers like two cloves of garlic," your thumb was placed between the two fingers. This resembled cloves of garlic or the hoof of the devil. Or, your thumb and two middle fingers held down while the remaining two fingers stood up like the *corna di lu diavulu*, the horns of the devil. Hoping this action would repel evil and stop the evil doer. Even if someone said how nice or pretty you were, this could cause headaches, fever, or misfortune.

As Sicilians, we have many superstitions. No new shoes on the table, I don't know why. Bread is always placed upright to avoid providence from falling out. No cats near a baby, it would suck its breath away. If you married during the month of May you would not enjoy your bed quilt because this was to be Mother Mary's month. A new house

39

needed salt in the corners and with a new broom you were to sweep the old spirits out. A loaf of bread was to be left to harden in the kitchen cabinet and never, ever live without a box of salt or holy water.

This night, as we entered Mamma's apartment there was Donna Filomina removing and applying leeches to my uncle Jimmy's back. He was a cabinet maker and someone accidently hit him in the back with a piece of wood. His shoulder was an array of colors, green, purple, red and black. The leeches purchased from the pharmacy were alive in a jar. They were black and looked like worms as big as my pinky. She applied several and waited for them to pierce the skin. Frank said that they were called *sanguisuca* (blood suckers). He continued that they had 100 teeth on both ends and when full they would fall off and not need to feed again for a year. They were used to suck the bruised blood to eliminate blood clots. Fascinated, as if watching a horror film, I looked through my fingers, I'm going to look, I'm not going to look. This continued until Donna Filomina said *"veni, veni ccà, picciridda"* (come, come here little one). I felt as cold as a popsicle, and slunk backwards. Of course, BUMP, Frank, the scutch was there with a big smile.

Donna Filomina was always invited to everyone's festivities for fear that she would be insulted and put a curse on you. Never did we see or hear about her family, strange.

The butcher on the ground floor was in a constant battle with her calling her a *strega*, witch, with no mystical powers. One day he called her a rabid dog (*cani raggiata*). Mamma told us that the butcher shop was crowded and so there were many witnesses when Donna Filomina lifted her crooked finger and pointing at the butcher said "I'll show you who is a dog, perhaps if you walk on all four legs you'll watch your foul mouth and treat me with respect". Lo and behold, the next day the shop was closed. In the war years of the 1940's no one closed their shop unless they were dead. As was the custom, we would have seen a spray of flowers on the door with a purple ribbon announcing a man had died. The story was, the butcher fell out of bed, hurt his back which forced him to crawl on his hands and knees to the bathroom. The butcher's wife told the neighbors that he asked for Donna Filominas' forgiveness. This new proof cemented everyone's suspicion, beware, she was *La Strega*.

Now she was openly sort after for the removal of *lu Mal'uocchiu*, the evil eye. As for marriage problems, a disloyal husband was unsuspectedly given a few droplets of his wife's monthly occurrence stirred into his black coffee. A wife with a wondering eye soon found a bouquet with certain herbs on her pillow. Whispers of *La Strega* on the rooftop baring her breast and baying at the full moon became part of everyday conversation.

Fortunate for me she was a real mother witch and brought my scary fairytales to life. Did she fly on a broom, cook with bones of rats and frogs? Who taught her? Who was she? Was she ever a little girl like me?

Curiosity soon replaced my fear; I watched her hands and listened when she spoke. Once, my brother hurt his ankle so she took oil from her apron pocket, gently lifted his foot and began to rub the sprain away. She noticed me next to her, took my hands and guided them on his ankle. She said "close your eyes, now, feel and see with your hands, find the knot in the muscle and massage it like this," and I did. Frank jumped up and did a little dance.

Soon fairytales became a fond memory and so did she. I never knew where she came from and can't remember when she left.

As Frank would say whooo whooo.......

One Never Knows

Every Sunday, Bushwick Avenue in Williamsburg resembled the Fifth Avenue Easter parade. The year was 1948. Now that the war was over, many of the immigrants' children married and moved away. But every Sunday, all dressed up, they returned just to have dinner and visit with friends and family.

Sophia and Marco were a young couple in love still living with their parents. As they walked arm-in-arm, stopping to say hello, people were captivated by their good looks. She was a young blonde girl with wavy hair surrounding her porcelain-skinned face. Her slim figure was enhanced by a flowy floral dress with matching hat and shoes and she was never without crisp, white gloves. He was as handsome as Errol Flynn in the 1948 movie Don Juan in an Italian, tailored pinstripe suit and black, hand-sewn leather shoes. He was quite dashing. Together, they walked with pride and confidence. It was said by the women of the neighborhood as they tittered, "hopefully Sophia will be able to get near the mirror when they wed."

Their nuptials would take place in June. Their families often remarked how beautiful their grandchildren would be. June came and the bride and groom on the cake topper took second place to Sophia and Marco.

When someone gets married, Sicilians immediately start to sound like baby chicks, "peep peep." "Are you having a baby? When? How come not yet?"

One day in the barber shop Marco was asked, "Marco, how are you doing in the baby department?" His answer took everyone by surprise. "Of course, I want only a son. If it's a girl, I'll throw her out the window. A man without a son to carry on his name is worthless." Some of the men laughed nervously while others nodded in agreement. Marco's words were soon spread up and down the street. Sophia heard his remarks from her mother before Marco came home. When asked, he didn't deny what he had said.

Two years have passed since Marco made his heartfelt statement. Mamma, her three daughters, my father and I stand behind the brown, wooden Venetian blinds. Today is the day they will come to take Sophia away. We all stop mid-sigh and catch our breath at the sight of the white ambulance that parks in the bus stop in front of her house. We gaze across at Sophia's window and see that it is still closed, shade drawn way down. At once, everyone begins to talk about the past events. We listen as my Aunt's story takes us by surprise. It seems that Sophia was pregnant and was going to tell Marco when he got back that day in 1948. Devastated, she attempted to rid herself of her unborn child. My Aunt continued to describe the bloodbath, wire hangers, and Sophia's broken-hearted mother. Sophia had confided to her mother, "I would prefer to never be a mother than to have him leave me. If it's a girl, it will have been all my fault. Mama, help me fix it so that Marco will never know." Her mother became her constant and only companion. Neighbors were occasionally asked, "Please, watch Sophia for a few minutes as I shop, for she has fallen into a deep despair and cannot be left alone." Sophia was drawn to the window like a moth to a flame. She begged, "Mama, please leave the window open." She knew her mother held the only key to the bars which kept her imprisoned. If only she was able to fly she might find solace, freedom, and peace. In a whisper or angry shouts, this wish was repeated over and over again. My father, being a man of nature, simply said, "why doesn't every man realize that it is the farmer's seed that denotes the crops that grow?" Being young, I didn't understand what this had to do with Sophia and Marco.

Gasping and placing their hands to their hearts, the women stepped closer to the window. Sophia, dreamlike, walked in slow motion. Two men in white coats and pants held each of her arms. A nurse in white with a navy-blue cape and white, starched cap led the way. Our eyes traveled upward to the third floor window, now open. There stood Sophia's mother, looking down and waving her granddaughter's hand "bye bye." Blonde, wavy hair surrounded her beautiful, little face as she blew kisses to her mommy. How sad — Marco refused to care for this little girl and her mother, choosing instead to return to Sicily at their time of need.

Making the sign of the cross, my family asked God to watch over their family as the ambulance pulled away.

The Braggart Loses His Voice

The war was becoming a dim memory. Music was heard as we walked up the stairs. The first floor was tuned to Carlo Buti, an Italian singer with a beautiful voice. He asked his love, "Do not forget me, *non ti scordar di me*." The next floor, Mamma was listening to Perry Como's, "If I Loved You". For us, the civilians, the war clouds dispersed, but not for the young men that came home from war.

This story is about a young man named Johnny. He suffered through the horror of war, seeing his best friend killed. With so many men returning, jobs were scarce and transition to civilian life, difficult. He was a gentle and thoughtful soul. During his army days, he remembered always to send souvenirs back to his mother and sister. Their favorite, a fringed satiny sentimental pillow that said "Mother" and a grass hula skirt for his sister. I was excited when his sister told me to try it on.

The men at the social club understood how hard it was to be an army man and then return home as if still a boy. They treated him with respect. Except Nardo who was a harsh, loud, obnoxious braggart, who would constantly poke at Johnny's shoulder. He was always telling him of his smart and wonderful daughter. "You call yourself a man? As I see it you're not. My daughter makes so much money that she is able to buy me anything I desire. Look at my new car. And how about this watch?" Johnny tried to walk away, but Nardo followed him and continued to taunt him. "Nardo, he said, tomorrow at noon, meet me here, I want to take you somewhere." This we children heard at the social club with my father.

A week had passed, and now my Uncle Lorenzo continued the story. My brother and I listened while climbing in and out of the window onto the fire escape, dangling our legs through the bars and going up and down the metal stairs. No one was concerned as they listened intently. It seems that Nardo and Johnny went to Manhattan. Entering an elegant building, they took the elevator to the top floor. A beautiful woman answered the door and kissed Johnny on the cheek. Welcoming them both in, she handed them a book of pictures so they could choose a lady of the evening. Nardo was sweating as he opened the book at Johnny's insistence. And there it was a picture of a beautiful girl, his daughter. Nardo buckled and began to cry. He remained speechless.

The last thing Uncle Lorenzo heard was that Nardo, returning home, waited until his daughter went to sleep, and then cut off her long braid. In Nardo's small village in Sicily, this was done to show that a woman was promiscuous. Women's uncut hair was a sign of virtue, faithfulness and femininity which they wove into a crown upon their head. I fingered my hair and took a deep breath, taking in what I had just heard.

A New Adventure

"Oh, Mommy, Mommy, please, let me go with them. Daddy, tell her it's okay." Looking at my father she waited until he nodded his head yes. Helping me on with my coat, a scarf and gloves, my mother said "Now remember, only as much as your thumb nail, okay?"

My father and brother held my hands and tried to protect me from the whipping wind and snow. Sliding across Bushwick Avenue down to Broadway, a quick turn and we were passing all the stores decorated for Christmas, 1945. There it was the giant candy cane. In front of *Patrinu*'s barber shop a barber pole, with its red and white twirling stripes, which I was told meant that the barber performed small surgeries. In Sicily, they would hang a bloodied cloth from a pole to signify this. The two large shop windows were covered in a fog; we could only see shadows from outside.

Our arrival was announced by a small bell above the door. The shadows we had seen were men sitting playing *scopa* and checkers, while Sicilian music was playing. The *Patrinu*, (godfather) was cutting someone's hair when he noticed us. We waited for him to finish and walked over. Smiling and bending down he kissed my cheek, took my hand and said "*Signorina, benevenuta* (welcome little miss), what can I do for you this evening?" "A haircut, please," I said. He swooped me up and placed me on a board high on the arms of the barber chair. He took a cape and with great flare he swirled the cape around my neck. He resembled a matador ready to face *el toro,* the bull. This was so exciting, this was all new to me since my uncle always cut our hair at home.

With slender scissors that he rapidly opened and closed and a rat-tail comb that looked like a half comb and pointed end which was used to section ladies hair, he waited for my instructions. Sitting tall and looking in the mirror I said, "take off only as much as my thumbnail." His hands moved quickly and little sprouts of hair flew around. Through the mirror I could see everything behind me. The store was large with a black painted tin ceiling with the same design as the one in my grandmother's kitchen. The walls, dark green, and the floor little black and white tiles just like my bathroom floor, eight barber chairs with barbers dressed in white coats. Their customers were being served with haircuts or a shave that consisted of a warm towel, a white soapy lather mixed in a cup with a brush and the use of a straight razor revealing baby soft skin. The barbers sharpened their straight razors against a brown leather strop hanging from the barber chair.

The air was filled with the smells of old spice, pomade, and talcum powder. But strongest of all was the sweet-scented smell of gardenia. My mother had a bottle of perfume called White Gardenia, a drop or two was put behind my ears on special days such as Christmas. Now that I was eight years old, I might be surprised by Santa Claus and receive my own bottle of perfume. As I daydreamed of all the gifts I was going to get, my uncle said, "*finitu*". Looking in the mirror my hair was as straight as spaghetti; my mother would definitely be heating the curling iron on the stove to make banana curls. As my uncle placed me back on the floor I said "*Grazii, Patrinu.*" Now it was my father and brother's turn to get their Christmas haircuts.

While I was waiting, I followed the smell of gardenia and found a windowsill filled with the most beautiful fragrant white wax-like gardenias, red and pink geraniums and best of all a perfect little tree filled with oranges. Continuing my adventure, I was introduced to Arturo from Tunisia, who was a dark skinned shoe shine man with hands that moved like a magician . I watched as he put polish from a little can on the shoe

and with a quick spit he shined the shoe with a dancing cloth held taught in his hands. My father called, my adventure was coming to an end, and a question remained, where in the world is Tunisia?

Cecelia Tumminello - De Luso

47

The Fig Tree

It was time to gather the figs. This was in preparation for company that would be coming on Saturday and Sunday. From the city they came for the fresh, cool air of the *campagna*. Fresh picked figs, vegetables, grapes and peaches were always in abundance on the dining room table.

Climbing the fig tree, I was guided by my grandmother's gnarly stick, an extension of her fingers. With taps at my ankles, the directions continued. "There, there! Move to the left, now place this foot to the right!" As I climbed, the bees were annoyed to leave the sweet nectar that looked like liquid gold coming from the overripe figs. These I was told to eat, to shoo the bee away and eat the untouched side. Out of my mouth, the words tumbled like rocks in a landslide. "Mamma, the bees will bite me." She said, "who's bigger and smarter: you or the bee? Now continue up the tree." Wow! Poking my head through the dense green canopy of the fig tree, I saw them. "*Mamma! Talìa, talìa* (look, look) – *li gemelli* (the twins)!" As I stretched over the top, she yelled, "be careful!" My hands grasped the prize: two beautiful perfectly-shaped light green plump figs. The tip resembled pursed lips that had been kissed pink by the sun. Mamma and I had watched these figs mature for several days. Happily, we had rescued them before the blackbirds, bees and ants got to feast on them. My scrawny seven year-old legs began to tremble as I started to descend. As I leaned forward to drop the figs to my grandmother, she said, "No, no, drop one. The other you eat. It's your prize for being brave and reaching the top."

I ate the fig and began to look around, imagining myself on a submarine, looking through a periscope – words we learned because of the war years. To my left stood manicured rows of vegetables and flowers which had been lovingly tended by my mother and father. The outhouse, water pump and grape arbor that was attached to the garage for dining outdoors (*al fresco*) looked small. "Wake up, it's too early to fall asleep! We have more work to do," my grandmother announced. As I continued to pick and gently drop the figs, she placed them stem-up in the egg cartons. The cartons were saved and brought from Brooklyn for the purpose of protecting each perfect fig as it chilled in the ice box. They were also used to carry eggs back from the chicken lady up the road.

Any mention of the egg cartons brought forth Mamma's story of the chicken lady. You see, several times a week Mamma, Frank and I would go with our egg cartons to buy eggs. The lady would take our cartons and return with the fresh-laid eggs. Mamma would smile and pay, and off we would go. The last time we went, Frank kept insisting, "*Mamma, veni, veni ccà!*" As Mamma went to the back of the chicken coop, she saw the lady unloading eggs from a truck. On the truck's door it said "Farm-Fresh Eggs from New Jersey." Placing her finger to her lips for silence, she smiled and paid for the eggs and we left. Frank and I questioned why she didn't say anything. "Well," she said, "now we know her secret – and we will only use her and her eggs when it's convenient for us."

The Real World - 1945

It was August 14th, 1945. Normally we'd be *in campagna* but we were home for a family wedding. Frank and I had no indication that this very day would go down in history.

Every morning, my mother listened to American music and sang along as she did her housecleaning. Strangely, we heard the Italian news on — this was usually reserved for my father when he got home at six o'clock. The newscaster, with urgency in his voice, spoke of President Truman, Hitler, and Hirohito – all names familiar to us from school and the gatherings of elders.

All week we heard about the end of the war. Was it going to end peacefully? Would we be safe here? Would the Japanese retaliate? My father had told us that in Manhattan, the store owners were boarding up their windows in anticipation of the celebrations. My aunt worked in the garment district. She said that the machine operators were saving scraps of fabric to throw out the windows like confetti if there was a parade.

Returning to school in September, we would no longer have to hide under our desks when we heard the air raid siren. At home, we huddled in a safe corner with the shades drawn and lights-out until the all clear siren sounded. For Christmas, we had each received a Rayovac pen light so that we could still finish our homework with no excuses. That evening, my father returned home, excited that the war would end. That night, as we did every Tuesday, we were going to mamma's house. Quickly, we got into the car. We lived on Hancock Street in the Bushwick section of Brooklyn. The street consisted mostly of two-family houses in a neat row. The front windows were usually kept closed. Shades and blinds were normally down with curtains drawn. That night, from our car, we noticed that the usually empty street seemed chaotic with open windows and people milling about. Our neighbors were all discussing what they expected to happen before the end of the night.

Reaching mamma's house, the tenements were as usual. Windows were open with curtains flying out and people extending their upper bodies to see who was down on the street. The stores and streets were filled with people. The noise was louder than usual. With Saint Catherine's hospital and the police station a few blocks away, flashing lights, sirens and speeding cars never ended. On the corner, the subway station was always alive with people coming or going. The trolley car ran in front of her house, adding to the chaos. Mamma's apartment also had its front windows open. We called them our "window on the world." Frank and I were always mesmerized by the activities down on the street. Each of us had a favorite pillow that we put on the window ledge and, with our feet planted on the floor, leaned out as far as we could. The organ grinder played music while his monkey, dressed in a blue jacket, danced and tipped his little red hat for coins. A push cart filled with blocks of ice covered in a dirty burlap cloth stopped and waited for customers. The ice man used a scoop with razor-sharp teeth to scrape at the block. The cup of shaved ice was then covered with a flavor of your choice — orange, cherry, or lemon.

That night, everyone was out. The fortune teller was there with his cards in a box, and his bird — which picked a card just for you — was there too. I found him to be fascinating, until someone told me that the bird's wings were broken so that it couldn't fly away. From then on, I looked at the man with angry eyes. People were gathering in groups, smoking and talking. Their hand gestures seemed more exaggerated tonight.

We were called to dinner and as we sat around the table, my Uncle Jimmy's ear was close to the radio. He was the first to hear President Truman make his official announcement at seven o'clock. Japan had surrendered — the war was, essentially, over.

The family began to clap and cry. My parents were laughing and hugging each other. My grandmother and aunt were dancing round and around. At that moment, a strange roar came from the street. In unison, my family rushed down the stairs. We were told to look out the window instead. When we looked below us, people were shoulder to shoulder. Car horns were blaring. Pots and pans — as if it was New Year's Eve — were banging. Firecrackers were going off. Every window was now flung open and people, like ants, were pouring out of the subway stairs. Frankie looked at me and said "let's go." We flew out the door, leaving our "window on the world" so that we could join the real world of happiness and jubilation.

As we went out the front door, we were stopped by the large group of men, women and children, sobbing and wailing. Sounds of agony were filling our ears and made us cry. I was eight; Frank was twelve. With arms stretched up to the sky, the Yiddish, the Polish and the Italians were all blaspheming against their gods in their native tongues, each asking what sense this war had made – and why he had allowed it.

In the crowd stood the young man who came back blind, tethered to his mother by a belt so he would not get lost. The crippled young soldier with one leg was there also. Young Johnny, who would drop to the ground and cover his head whenever he heard a loud noise, was also present.

Frank and I stood there, crying and quivering like two reeds in a storm. At that moment, our childhood innocence was lost. We had truly entered the real world.

Frankie, Louie and Frank, influenced by the war.

Always the Child

Sunday was always a fun-filled, busy day. My parents believed Sunday should be for God and family. After church, my father, brother, and I would go to grandma's house. This was a time for my father and his three brothers, her four sons, to come together and talk with men friends about politics, hunting, and fishing. Grandma would serve us fresh baked rolls with little bellybuttons on top. As children we knew that the older we were, the darker our coffee. Her daughters-in-law would be home to prepare for their families' dinner or plans that they had made. Nice weather would find us at the stables in City Line, for me a pony ride and Frank to ride the horses. My father's choice was the water's edge. My mother's favorite was visiting a new church or eating an impromptu lunch at a newly discovered park.

Today my father was excited to show off our new car to his mother and brothers. Yesterday my father left his 1937 DeSoto, with the beautiful chrome hood ornament of a lady with an upturned face, at the car dealership. The distortion of our face and body as we cleaned the chrome on our old car made us look like a circus-sideshow. Today we rode in our new 1949 DeSoto, black, shiny and sleek. Sitting in the back seat, I felt rich.

As we pulled up, we were car number four. Grandma waved and the brothers smiled. Not many cars were parked on Woodbine Street. Not many neighbors had four sons that came every Sunday. My grandmother's bosom surely swelled with pride.

Entering the house each kissed their mother and discreetly handed her five dollars. Each received a pat and a kiss in return. As curious children, we stood at the end of the hall and looked to see if the money she tucked into the top of her house apron would fall out the bottom. Nope, it never happened.

Around the table everyone had been served. Happily, my grandmother returned to stirring her Sunday sauce. Uncle, the eldest and most outspoken, stood up. In a low voice he said to his brothers, "Watch this." The three brothers shook their heads and warned him, "Harry, don't!" Smiling he began, "Mama, I read that in Alaska when the parents get old, the Eskimos (*l'Eschimesi*) put them on a big piece of ice and push them out to sea. Then the children don't have to take care of them." The words had fallen out of his mouth, and like smoke he could not retrieve them. When did he become such a dolt?

The room was now filled with silence. All I could hear was the sound of my heartbeat in my ears.

Oh! No! The warm sunny inviting kitchen filled with Sicilian Sunday smells, slowly became a frozen tundra. Even the sun tiptoed behind the clouds as she turned. Her five foot shadow now elongated on the wall with wooden spoon above her head. She transformed into Zeus, the Greek God with a thunderbolt raised in his hand.

The thunderbolt was thrown, whoosh! One word, "*maladucatu,*" which means ill mannered, rude, or ill bred. With a face as pale as plain boiled pasta, my uncle said "*Mama, mi dispiaci, pirdunami.*" (I'm sorry, forgive me) Impervious to his heartfelt words, she responded "Your wife waits, go home." Turning she resumed her stirring.

La famigghia Tumminello

Gathering our things we kissed her and said, "*A sa benedica.*" She responded, "*Addiu*" (goodbye), see you Sunday." When we told my mother, she said "Now it is between mother and son. A mother's heart breaks when a child is disrespectful, even if it is said in jest." Lesson learned. Now you would think that was the end. Not so, it was continued, as Sicilians always do. They forgive, but don't forget. At a time when you least expect it, the past situation rears its ugly head.

Sunday came and my father made the sign of the cross as we once again parked as car number four.

As conversation unfolded about children and parents, respect, and being too mouthy, my grandmother simply said "A mother can raise ten children, but ten children can't care for one mother." Not wanting a response, she simply asked, "Who wants more coffee?" Ah, now it had ended, let's eat.

New Home New Life

When you are 11 almost 12 you think you can say "I can stay home alone, don't worry, I'll just invite my friend to come over." Sounds good, but it never happened. My mother emphatically said "that's all your grandmother and aunts would have to hear that I left you alone, *Camina.* (walk)"

Saturday evening visits to someone, home from the hospital, a death in the family or just news and photos from Sicily were important and had to be shared and delivered in person. My parents were the ones with a car and so they became the mobile ambassadors and representatives of "The Family". Williamsburg in the 1950's was changing. And so we traveled to Maspeth, Middle Village, City Line and tonight, Howard Beach on the water.

Most of the older women who lost their husbands decided to move in with their daughters. The family unit became daughter, son-in-law, their children and the old lady with the black dress, black stockings and a shopping bag filled with money. This resulted from the sale of their stores or homes that they could no longer manage on their own. The lucky ones had an apartment in the basement with their own kitchen, but most had a bedroom and shared the rest of the house.

They believed and were told this would be a better life. Soon they found that independence and the social circle that kept them involved and interested in life was gone.

Signura Carmela had been uprooted and transported to Howard Beach. She explained that she did not leave the house very often for fear that if she fainted she would lay in the street with no one knowing who she was. Since moving in with her daughter she confided to my parents, I walk with two feet in one shoe. (*caminu cu dui pedi nta na scarpa*). I'm not *la patruna* (the owner) anymore.

As the conversation went on, I walked to what I thought was her china closet. This one piece of furniture always fascinated me. Everyone we knew had this special place to put their finest treasures. Often you would see *lu carrettu sicilianu*, the Sicilian cart adorned with images of kings and queens drawn by a horse with a magnificent plume. Sparkling pieces of Murano glass, figurines with skirts made of lace dipped in clay and fired at very high heat, they were called porcelain. A large array of

wedding favors given by a bride and groom as a thank you gift consisted of birds, figures and baskets. Each tied with little net bag which held three to five almonds. Sicilians believe that odd numbers are luckier. The three or five almonds, or *confetti* as we call them, were bitter almonds coated in white sweet sugar. These almonds symbolized the bitter-sweet sacrament of marriage. Five almonds represent health, wealth, happiness, fertility and long life. She had many music boxes and at Christmas time the light bulb was changed to blue to resemble the night sky for the nativity that took over the entire middle shelf. As little children, we were allowed to hold any object we wanted as she told us a story about it. This evening as I stood there, she came over and sadly said, "All of my treasures have been put in the attic. My daughter decided that my furniture was old and I had too much junk." We both stared at the lifeless stemware and dish after dish with one pattern. "It's too expensive to be used. It's just for show," she said. Her daughter entered, the smell of demitasse permeated the room, and the cookies we had brought were placed on the table. My family had brought and exquisite imported *Capo di Monte* basket of flowers as her new home gift. We knew she would appreciate, enjoy and display it with love.

Perhaps it would find a new home in the breakfront. Most likely it would be in her bedroom out of site of the new white French provincial furnishings where the new and old world would not clash.

Oh What a Breeze!

Today was Assembly Day when the principal came and we listened to many speeches. Our dress code was a navy blue pleated skirt and a white blouse. Underneath was always your undershirt the one with a little bow in the middle. Knee high socks, a cotton slip and Oh, a pair of slippery cotton candy pink bloomers. The elastic was a little loose but no time to change, the school bell would soon be ringing and Frank was yelling "You're going to make me late." Down the front stairs and we met up with Frank's classmates. They walked ahead of me as I was too busy looking at the trees and the new leaves, the dogs that barked saw me every morning but I quickened my step just in case they got out of the fence. Aah! *Primavera*, my attention was on the blue sky and fluffy clouds, as I took my next step, plop went my cotton candy bloomers. Shocked I stood still for a minute and then seeing everyone ahead of me I stepped out of them and ran. Not wanting anyone to know I ran up the stairs and to my classroom and realized what if I fell? What if we had a real fire and we had to climb down the ladder? All I could hear was my friends singing, "I see London, I see France, I see Cecelia's …whoops surprise, surprise no underpants."

The day was uneventful, no jumping rope or cleaning of the erasers. But when the dismissal bell rang, panic took over. Now everyone would know. What would I say? As we got closer those that were closest began to laugh. There they were in the street big and pink like a flag they were waving in the wind. My parents always said, "when in Rome do as the Romans do" and so I did. They pointed and laughed and so did I. Telling my mother, we both laughed ourselves silly and she said "Oh, what a breeze on such a beautiful day." "When you tell Mamma what do you think she will say?"

You see, Mamma said that the only shame was if we exposed our behinds. Not for real but as an expression. If we were to expose some family secrets, or something about ourselves that we did not want to get around. Sicilians and their families are protective of each other. This was to teach us that we should always protect our backs. We could see what was in front of us and able to defend ourselves, but not behind us. She would say, "Your best friend can become your worst enemy if she knows all your secrets. Measure your words. Think before you act. After all we are only human. *Lu Signuruzzu li cosi li fici dritti, vinni lu diavulu e li sturciù*. God made things straight but along came the devil and as usual twisted them. Words are the easiest things to twist. And, remember your tongue has no bones but it has the ability to break bones. *A lingua nun avi ossa ma rumpi l'ossa*."

Best Man-Uncle Jimmy and Maid of Honor - my mom Jennie.

New Year's Eve

"*Panza china voli riposu*," a full stomach needs rest. This proverb would not come to pass tonight. Lasagna and meatballs plus delicacies too numerous to mention brought groans and belly rubbing. Soon conversation was turned into laughter and discussion of serious card playing. The grown men jingled their change-filled pockets, chose their seats and broke the seal on a new pack of cards. Bowls of nuts were placed on the table. We, the cousins, also played games. We took the *nuciddi*, hazelnuts, to use in place of marbles. A circle drawn on a brown paper bag with one nut placed in the middle, we took turns trying to knock the *nucidda* out of the center.

Most children were told not to play with food. These were the times when we were encouraged to do so. Sea urchins, *rizzi di mari*, looked like a ball covered with hundreds of tubed feet with five teeth on their backside. Those that we ate were cut open with a pointed barber scissor. Opened alive, it revealed compartments filled with an orange substance with a texture creamier then fish roe. Their roe was actually the gonads and considered a delicacy. This we ate with a demitasse spoon, a few drops of vinegar and oil, lemon juice or just plain. The smell was that of a fresh ocean. My father's eyes would get pensive as he reminisced about Sicily's blue waters and his youth.

Tonight we learned how to place a wager. Again a brown paper bag cut open, a start line and a finish line were drawn. We chose three of the liveliest and freshest looking *rizzi*. We lined them up, they were sprinkled with salt which energized them or agitated them and they began to move slowly. As if watching a horse race, we placed our pennies and the men bet quarters on their favorite. We also did this with large white sea *babbaluci*. We took our winnings or moaned over our losses. With the race over, the men returned to their chosen seats and soon the room was engulfed in smoke. My cousins and I now began to search where we would sleep tonight. The words, "I call it", were heard as we each chose a couch, a chair, or were relegated to sleeping on coats on the floor. Tonight would be a family sleepover. Drinking and card playing would go on all night.

Our attention soon turned to the women who were laughing hysterically as grandma told the story of her *Cummari*. It seems that *La Cummari* dressed in her taffeta dressy-dress and *pilliccia*, fur stole, walked into the wedding hall with a piece of toilet paper stuck to the heel of her

60

shoe. *La Cummari* walked proud and tall as people pointed, thinking it was her great looks, until someone pointed to her shoe.

My grandmother was mainly a good listener, but tonight she was full of stories. I thought it was the spirit of the holiday, and then I noticed each of the ladies held a small glass of liqueur that my mother had made. With a gallon of alcohol, an eye dropper for her oils and essences, through a tiny funnel, she made her New Year's concoctions.

Everyone was having a good time and then, from the men's side of the table, you heard *porca miseria* (damn it), and the slam of a hand of cards someone was not happy with. Boisterous bravado turned to laughter and the card game continued.

The mantle clock, with no regard to the festivities was about to remind us of the beginning of a new year. With pots, pans, wooden spoons, and covers as cymbals, we counted down the minutes, "Bong 5, bong 4, 3, 2, 1 Happy New Year!" As we ran outside, the crunch of ice underfoot and falling snow that covered everything made our world look new. New Year's Day would once again be shared with family and anyone else that wished to join us. Our guests included all walks of life, from the *ruffiana*, the matchmaker, to the *beccamortu*, the undertaker. Today, time would have no meaning and so the proverb, *megghiu tardu ca mai*, better late than never prevailed.

     Filici Annu Novu —Happy New Year

Remember the Times

Remember the times you absentmindedly tried to cut a loaf of bread with the wrong side of the knife blade?

Or tried to eat soupy pasta and peas with a fork, too lazy to get a spoon?

Went out in the rain without a jacket, thinking soon the rain would stop?

These were the perfect times to be called Giufà. Sicilians using Giufà, with great affection, of course, would explain his existence. He was the town simpleton. Lazy at times and easily distracted, common sense was absent from his mind. You would be asked the question, "But who are you, Giufà?" (*ma cu sì, Giufà?*)

Giufà, comu lu penza, accussì lu fa. (the way he thinks it, he does it).

Now the stories would start:

One day Giufà's mother said, "Giufà, I need you to go to the pasture and tend to the sheep. Stay all day and return for dinner. For lunch I am giving you a loaf of bread, a small wheel of cheese and a big piece of fruit. This will keep your belly full (*panza china*)." Dinner time came and Giufà's mother heard him come down the path crying, "I'm hungry, I'm so hungry." His mother asked, "Why didn't you eat your lunch?" "Because," he said, "You forgot to give me a knife."

"Giufà, really?"

And then there was the story that prevented you from having an excuse for being late. It was Sunday, time to go to Church. "Giufà, are you ready?" "Giufà, where are your shoes?" "Giufà, hurry up!" In desperation, the mother said, "Giufà, when you are ready, pull the door and come to church (*tirati la porta dappressu*)." Mass began, communion finished, the priest gave his final blessing, and still no Giufà. Looking out the window she saw Giufà pulling the door behind him. "Giufà, what have you done?" "I pulled the door, like you said, and here I am!"

"Giufà, really, really?"

The Gilded Cage

It was soon to be Christmas and young people that had moved away would come to visit friends and family. The softness of her grey fox fur jacket against my cheek, the satin of her dress with matching shoes, bag and hat in dove grey, made her look like she could be in a fashion magazine or a Hollywood movie. Her name was Lucia; she was my mother's childhood friend. They had not seen each other for four years, since Lucia had moved to Chicago. She hugged me and said, "I'm going to take you to Chicago to be my little friend." Hearing this, I quickly stepped behind my mother's elbow, holding tightly onto her dress. Lucia hugged my mother and began to talk. As they moved to the front room, I followed.

There, she confided to my mother, all the jewels, furs and beautiful surroundings that Matthew had promised her came true. But what her family had said was also true — it seems they had advised her not to marry Matthew. Her life with him would be totally different, they said. Her looks, her actions and her every movement would be scrutinized. His bosses, friends and acquaintances had their own code of behavior. It was imposed not only on the men but also on their women. Having returned from World War II, Matthew was unable to adjust to civilian life. He tried, but the war years had weighed heavily on him. Having seen death daily and causing death of people he did not know overwhelmed him. Returning to the old neighborhood left a void in his heart. So many teenage friends were gone or returned broken. He had tasted the fast-paced life of money, power and after-hour clubs in the foreign countries where he was stationed. Life was unpredictable and he wanted to grab the world in his fist, he would say: "*Vogghiu pigghiari lu munnu nton pugnu.*" Lucia was blinded by the attention he paid to her. She no longer wanted to be part of her family; she regarded them uneducated, stagnant and immersed in the old world's ways. As peasants they worked the land and coming here they continued to work with fruits and vegetables. They felt blessed, fulfilled and safe among the people of their own town.

Just as she had accepted a new family, so did he; Matthew had become a soldier in a very different kind of family. Chicago's underground was open territory for gangs and corruption. Matthew chose gambling as his profession. She soon became his starry-eyed bride. Lucia confided that just to be able to go to the five-and-dime and buy lipstick without a bodyguard would now be her greatest treat. She said to my mother, "I would exchange all my riches for the peace of mind that at night, while I lay in bed, the turning of the key in the lock would guarantee my husband was coming home — and not someone he had lost me to in a card game." Sadness and tears followed as my mother tried to console her friend. Lucia's husband had returned. His voice boomed from the front door: "It's time to go, now." Checking her makeup and applying fresh lipstick, she lowered a veil over her red-rimmed eyes. With hugs and kisses and promises to return, she quickly left.

My mother looked at me and said, "remember always – nothing is more important than the freedom to think and act on your own. Lucia may have everything, but she is like a bird in a gilded cage. And when she sings, she sings a mournful song."

After their Christmas visit, we heard that the New Year would bring Matthew the advancement he so desperately wished-for and earned. Holidays came and went; Lucia never visited again.

A Love Denied

"Zia Lena, (Aunt), why did you never marry?" "Ah, Cecelia, such a serious face. You see, my true love and I, our outer ways set us apart. The cross I wear, the skull cap he." We asked ourselves, "How can this be?" "Alone apart, we were whole together, I a girl of 23, he a boy of 27. Cultural worlds divide us and yet one heart unites us."

The world is vast and yet minute. World War II was raging. The year was 1943. What will they say? Together alone, we hold hands on the Brooklyn ferry line, no one here knows us, no one here cares. On land and shore our worlds collide. Religion tells us to abide, charity, love, and forgiveness.

His mother said, "Marry her, Moshe my son, you will be dead to me." My mother said, "I will die, and you'll wear black." Both, with voices that rose, "never, never, this love can't be, what will our people say?"

No place to hide, no place to go. Alone together, we would not survive.

Separate days were soon to be. "Angelina, I'll dry your tears and Moshe, I'll wipe yours." With tear rimmed eyes, we ask, "why love, why love that cannot be? A heart should know what felt right was wrong. Human we are, if cut we bleed. No one would hear us, no one believes us. This love is right, this love is just, when *La famiglia Costa.* not accepted, it becomes a curse."

"Torn apart, families hate and fear astounds us. With lips that quivered and crying eyes, we vowed to love no other. We chose to walk, and walked our empty road forever."

"Alone perhaps, yet never lonely, you see his love is always with me."

Sicilian proverb: Better to be alone than in bad company "*Megghiu sula ca mali accumpagnata.*"

A Magical Night

"Hurry, Frank, it's time to go, grab the chestnuts, it's starting to snow." The chestnuts were sputtering in the potato baker. The old stovetop baker was the best place to roast them. A little cross cut on the rounded top allowed the steam to escape to avoid the explosion they could cause.

"Quick, put on your galoshes." Frank was struggling with the buckles on his galoshes; there was always one or two that didn't match. My boots were white, fit over my shoes and with a simple zip, zip, I stood waiting and waiting. Frank looked like he had "*li pedi di papira*" (the feet of a duck). The chestnuts, cooked and hot, were put in our pockets to keep our hands warm and have something to eat on the way.

Slipping and sliding, we got to the elevated Hancock Street train station on Broadway to meet up with our father. The stores were decorated with lights, garlands and beautiful window dressings. Standing on the street looking up the stairs, all we could see were shoes, pants, and coats. Then our daddy's black shiny wing tipped shoes stepped down. With a smile on his face, he said, "Are you and Frank ready to pick out the biggest, tallest Christmas tree?" Jumping up and down I said, "It has to be the most beautiful tree ever!" We shared our chestnuts with our father and went on to the empty lot that was now transformed into a fairyland forest. The smell of pine, colored lights, and trees of all sizes surrounded us. In the center stood a large metal drum with a roaring fire, and sparks that looked like miniature fireworks.

Mr. Jack, the Christmas tree man, said, "Do you like this one?"

"No it's too skinny."

"How about this one?"

"No, this one only has branches on one side. Remember Daddy, it must look beautiful on all sides."

Looking at Mr. Jack, I told him that our Christmas tree stood in the middle of the room. Then I saw the most beautiful tree with little pinecones on it. I looked at my father and brother and soon the tree had been tied up with rope so that Frank and Daddy could carry it home.

My father always said, "Remember where you are, now take a deep breath and enjoy the smell of pine." "Ah, *sciariati tutti l'arvuli*" (smell the trees). Our senses were now filled with the smells of Christmas.

My father and brother decided that pulling the tree was easier and this created a path on the new fallen snow. The few cars on an otherwise busy Bushwick Avenue were covered in snow, traveling slowly, and leaving what looked like red ribbons from their taillights. Only the sound of tire chains could be heard. It was strange to see the reflection of the headlights that were still painted half black because of the war years. This was done so that they could not be seen brightly from airplanes if we were invaded by the enemy.

My mother was all bundled up, waiting on the front stoop with the doors wide open, to allow the big tree in. She guided the tree into the center of the living room. The ropes were cut and the tree stood big and bold. Impatiently, my brother and I started pulling at the boxes of decorations. "No, no, children! Your father has worked all day, and dinner will come first." My father's part was done; the rest was up to us.

Frank would climb the ladder and add the lights to the tree. My mother and I would decorate using chains made from construction paper, lacey angels, paper birds, and fragile Christmas balls of silver, gold and red. "Let's not forget the tinsel and bubbling candlelights, they are my favorite." The finishing touch was the beautiful angel on top.

A white sheet was put under the tree so that we could create our nativity scene (*presepe*). Ours was not the traditional stable. My father believed that the holy family took shelter in a cave to await the birth of Jesus. This idea came from working as a young boy in Sicily as an apprentice in a blacksmith shop. There, he would fix the carts of the traveling astronomers and astrologers, listening to their stories as he worked. He built us a cave out of metal and green painted rocks, which was placed on the sheet under our tree. Small empty boxes placed under the sheet created a hillside setting. Shepherds, their lambs and goats were placed as though they were descending. On the right, the Magi, those mysterious kings from the east, Caspar, Melchior and Balthazar, carrying gifts looked regal and lifelike in their robes. We also had a dark skinned boy that held a gold cord attached to the camel. An angel and star was placed to guide them from above. Lastly, Mary and Joseph, a cow and a donkey were placed on real hay inside the cave. Jesus remained wrapped in a white handkerchief that was placed in an old soft sock. After midnight, when we returned home from grandma's house on Christmas Eve, Frank and I would place Jesus in the manger. Out of the closet Frank pulled a heavy box containing his Lionel train set. This was the last thing to complete our tree. The tree was lit, the train blew its whistle, and we sat in awe of this magical night. To each other we said… "BUON NATALE"

Christmas Eve

A communal spirit had been going on all week. Piled high were trays of cucciddati, fig cookies topped with rock sugar and colored nonpareils, and mounds of *pignolata*, small pinky size sweet fried dough, drizzled with honey and covered with multicolored sprinkles.

Aunt Pauli, my father's sister, was in charge of holiday baking. Aunt Pauli would come home from working at the dress factory and begin immediately. As usual she would put on her apron and forget to take off her hat. Her *scanaturi*, (wooden kneading board) was covered in flour with a well in the center where she dropped her eggs, vanilla and sugar. With strength and know-how she used her *mattarello*, (rolling pin). Soon it was turned into a smooth circle of dough and divided amongst the helpers.

Tonight was Christmas Eve and the culmination of family togetherness. I wondered how many we were, I couldn't say. The front door was left unlocked and all were welcomed tonight. Family, friends, and in-laws celebrated together. Family economics were put on hold. This was a Sicilian, family style Christmas Eve, a time to give thanks and praise to Baby Jesus. God was nourishment for the spirit and soul. Soon the three fishes, which symbolize the biblical three wise men, or seven fishes, the seven biblical days of creation would be prepared. God's favorite number seemed to be seven, the seven biblical days of creation, the seven deadly sins, the seven sacraments, and the seven colors in the rainbow.

From the Fulton Fish Market, we brought back eels so fresh that when they were cut to be fried they continued to wiggle. Live octopus was immersed in boiling water until its eight arms curled up, and was cooked, cooled and chopped into a cold fish salad. Fried smelts, small enough to be eaten bones and all, *baccalaru*, salted cod in light sauce and *scungilli, calamari* and shrimp cooked in a devilishly hot sauce was then ladled over five pounds of linguini.

Homemade wine and draft beer, which was brought from the local bar in a metal container, was enjoyed throughout the night. The *cosi duci,* sweets, were brought out while the women chatted and the men played cards. Soon my grandmother's mantle clock spoke up, bonging twelve times, signifying that it was now Christmas Day. The cooking began again, now preparing a delectable and bountiful meat meal, sausage, rabbit, and salad.

As the night wore on, we returned home in the wee hours of the morning. We placed Baby Jesus in our manger and then slept for a few hours. Now we would exchange gifts and attend Christmas Mass. Dinner today would be at Momma's home.

At Christmas Mass, the walls trembled with the sound of organ music. Snowflakes, brushed from collars and the sound of stomping feet to remove the snow was all around us. *Paisani* greeted each other and oohed and aahed with *pizzicuni e vasuni*, (pinches and big kisses) on our red cold cheeks. "Buon Natale" was heard in hushed voices as we found our seats.

The church was decorated with special gold embroidered cloths edged with handmade lace on the altar, flowers everywhere you turned, and life-size statues depicting the nativity with animals so realistic, you had to stop yourself from petting one.

After church, at Mamma's home, the table was set with one extra place for a weary traveler or unexpected guest. Holidays remind us we are always connected and never alone.

And the tradition continues.

Wishing you all the Joys of Christmas and many Blessings in the New Year…..

Water Color By Cecelia

70

A Virtuous Woman

A million conversations, who to listen to? After dinner at my grandmother Cecelia's house, before coffee and sweets, the women gathered on one side of her kitchen. The men settled into a card game of Rummy, Pinochle or Blackjack, on the other side. As children we would go into the living room to play games, talk, giggle and laugh, prodded often by the older cousins to look up "dirty words" in the dictionary. We would run back and forth to our mothers to nestle, complain or just to listen. Their conversations would be about foods, fashion, how much money to give for an upcoming wedding or whispered off-colored jokes that provoked laughs and wide eyed tell-all looks.

Lately, as "young ladies" of 11 to 16 years old, my cousins and I spent more of our time in the kitchen. Here we asked questions, how will I know my true love? When can I date?

How did you meet uncle? Will I become pregnant if a boy kisses me?

Our questions and female advice was given "the Sicilian way" through an old time story, or more often, the third party method. The proverb, "*parrari cu me figghia, ascutari a me nora.*" Loosely translated, I speak to you my daughter, but my intentions are for my daughter-in-law to learn a lesson. Today my grandmother Cecelia decided her four granddaughters all named after her needed to learn about virtue. Looking towards my eldest cousin as if the story was intended only for her, a wave of her hand and a tone of drama and conviction in her voice, she began the saga, "A Virtuous Woman."

Maria Theresa was preparing for a sleep filled with dreams of her prince. Mother had told her that although she was a young lady from a poor family, she had a most precious gift reserved only for her prince. She understood and promised to protect her virtue.

Humming alone in her room, lace curtains billowing, and crickets singing, she brushed her long thick curly hair. She pinned her hair up and it glistened in the moonlight. Startled by a low murmur coming from the open window, she turned and saw Him. His red face engorged with passion, and his lecherous smile was frightening. In a low growl he said, "Maria Theresa, your innocence has brought me here, it is time for you to be mine." Pulling the combs out, her hair cascaded and encircled her like a shroud. She began to weave to and fro. The devil pounced, reached for her slender waist and became entangled in her hair. Furiously, he retreated with only hairs in his hands. Loudly she sang, "Never, Never will you have your way with me. My prince will receive his prize."

The devil exhausted and weakened from his unrewarded attempt at passion slithered out of the window. Maria Theresa heard a low, wounded animal sound. Was it truly the devil? (*diavulu*), was it the wind? (*ventu*) or a dream? (*sognu*) Rushing to the window she saw a dark figure outlined by the full August moon and heard his eerie moan. "Ooonly a virgin can outsmart the spirit of evil."

The moral of this story, "when a woman wants to keep her virtue, not even the devil can succeed."

Story as told by my grandma Cecelia in the Spring. . .

Cousins.

Teenager 1952

A new family moved in next door: mother, father and a teenage son. Both of our mothers agreed, let's introduce the two teenagers. My mother announced that, "Jack's mother invited you to visit this afternoon. Just talk and get to know each other."

Talking to Jack was like talking to a rolled up rug, (*tappitu*). There was no beginning and no end.

His mother called from the kitchen, "Jack, see if she wants something to eat."

"No, thank you," I said. Jack looked at me and replied, "She was talking about the dog."

Quickly I excused myself and went home. Telling my mother how good an idea it was to meet Jack. She replied "Patience! he's young and foolish."

Mamma

"Mamma, what is in this box, *petri* (rocks?) " Ah, dear grandson, we here in America are privileged to send things to the old country. I am sending clothes, material and even a *grattalora* (grater), *sculapasta* (pasta strainer), and I never forget a *giucattulu* (toy) for my godson Giovanni. Since you're the same age, yes, yes I bought one for you and looking at me, and you too. In the corner they will find a little money for the holiday."

She labored to pack these boxes, wrapping them in brown paper, tying them with strong twine, with the address printed boldly in black crayon, Castelvetrano, Sicily. Helping her, we would walk the many blocks to the post office. This continued for many years.

As time passed Frank and I continued our life's path. He graduated from Aviation High School and the Academy of Aeronautics. He pursued his education while working at Idlewild Airport. He would return to Aviation High School as a teacher. For now, he planned his first airplane trip, destination, Rome. Hearing this, Mamma, with great excitement went to her bureau. Under the hand-crocheted scarf, next to a wedding invitation, some money in case of an emergency or a house call from the doctor, she took the letter that said Giovanni was a respected lawyer now living in Rome.

"Frank, you must visit him. Here is his address, fifty dollars, and his photo. Don't forget to give him the money, but only when the time is right. Careful not to embarrass him, we don't want to make a *mala figura*." (bad show).

"But Mamma, I don't know him." The photo he held showed a slender young man with a shock of black hair, an aquiline nose and a pencil thin mustache. With a smile she said, "now you know him, he is a man, *comu iddu ti sona, accussì tu canti*." (The way he plays that's the way you sing.)

"Let him direct the conversation, if he talks of riches or poverty you follow. The weather or your trip, you lead. If he begins to talk about Sicilian politics, be quiet, listen and learn. You learn nothing from hearing your own voice."

In Rome, my brother was met by Giovanni who extended an invitation to his home. Giovanni's home was a small palace with servants. At the push of a button the wall slid open exposing decanters, glasses, liquors and wine that shimmered in the sunlight. Together they toasted Mamma's health and past generosity. Late into the afternoon they chatted and laughed like two old friends about Mamma and the *paisani* that had moved to America. Frank drank his coffee, ate his *duci* (sweets) and bid farewell to his host

As a true Sicilian gentlemen, so as not to cause an awkward situation, he took the fifty dollars from his right pocket folded it neatly, placing it in his left pocket, solution, a gift for Mamma. And so, from Rome, he brought and placed on her shoulders, *un beddu sciallu* (a beautiful shawl.) Her weathered hands held tightly to her gift. Her eyes glistened as she heard about the toast to her health and generosity. The smile on her face was worth all the treasures in Rome.

I smiled as Mamma fingered her shawl, thinking, whenever you asked her if there was anything she needed or wanted, she would reply, *"Nun mi bisogna nenti, mancu na cascia cu li denti"*. ("I don't need anything, not even a set of false teeth.")

Outrageous

Graduation in June was soon approaching. The calendar read 1954. Being a senior meant yearbook pictures, class rings, dances, and little romances. We were kept in a state of high anxiety. Nothing prepared us for all the arrangements we needed for the prom at the Statler Hotel in New York. My high school, Franklin K. Lane High School, was a sprawling, four-story building with one of the largest Olympic swimming pools and beautiful football fields. Built next to the Cyprus Hills' cemetery, we were assured of quiet, non-complaining neighbors. Because I chose French as my foreign language, I had to travel on the elevated train from my home in the Bushwick section of Brooklyn – an hour of travel time away. Coming from Junior High School PS 85 to this massive school took some adjusting. At the time it was built, this high school was the largest in the world. It measured one quarter mile on each floor. The cafeteria was filled with narcotics officers on a daily basis. Drugs were rampant in the 1950's, as well as the unfortunate race riots that never seemed to end. Drug dealers were always lurking around, but we continued with our studies. The secretarial group I was with ate standing up near the exit sign. As tables, benches, punches, and books went flying and the roar of chaos came closer, we returned to our classrooms. My only encounter with the "tough girls" was on the staircase. My long hair was yanked. I was pushed and my books and I went tumbling down. Telling my mother, she simply said, "Tomorrow, you must be more observant and use a different staircase." And I did. Problem solved.

At home, the night's discussion was all about the prom. The young man that had asked me to go with him found that when he checked his pockets, all he could come up with were four dead moths and some dust. The expenses of prom tickets, the limo and a tuxedo overwhelmed him. Two weeks before prom night, stuttering and stammering, he said "I'm so sorry." Now to find a solution. My beautiful, white, strapless cocktail-length dress with the blue velvet sash, dusted with silver glitter, three crinolines and strappy silver high-heels stood ready. Sicilian Proverb: *"Com'è beddu lu pitrusinu! Vinni lu jattu e ci pisciau"* How beautiful is the parsley – along came the cat and pissed on it. Anyone joining us for dinner was welcomed to the open forum where we aired problems and found solutions. This evening, it was my brother Frank's girlfriend who insisted that a girl should not miss her prom. She suggested that Frank take me to the prom instead. He would have completed his army's basic training at Fort Dix, New Jersey and would be home in plenty of time. How outrageous — going to the prom with your brother! "I have a better idea," I said to my mother. "Let's give the young man the money needed for tickets, a tuxedo and other expenses." My mother listened to all I had to say and remarked, "*Pippina è tutta nticchiata – e unni è Pippinu*? (Peppina is all dressed up – and Peppino, where is he?)" My mother continued, "And then you can tie the strings." Another Sicilian riddle – where was she going with this one? My mother had a great sense of humor that was occasionally tinged with sarcasm — just enough to keep things interesting. "I give up, Mom." "Well," she said, "Now that you've dressed and stuffed money in the puppet's pockets, you need the strings to make him dance to your music." I agreed. Bad idea; back to Frank.

Prom night arrived and my brother looked handsome in his tuxedo. My corsage was a beautiful white orchid which I'd only seen in bridal bouquets. Arriving by limo, I felt like a starlet. Entering the vastness and grandeur of the Statler Hotel was breathtaking. The flashing lights of the mirror-ball made my head spin. This was a moment I would always remember. Each piece of mirror reflected the past, the present, and the unforeseen. I was surrounded by people and yet alone in my sense of wonder for the future. The adult world waited, and I was ready; never would I hesitate to experience life. Although the night was not filled with the expectations of a seventeen year old— a stolen kiss, sweet nothings whispered in my ear, or the touch of a young man's fingers on the small of my back as we danced — it was truly outrageous.

Unexpectedly, the night unfolded as though life's winding highway was a straightaway, all signposts down. No stop signs, yields or dangerous curves ahead. It simply ended as an unforgettable joyride.

Thanks, brother.

The Classes of January–June 1954

cordially invites you to its

Senior Prom

on Saturday, May 15, 1954

at the Hotel Statler

Dinner served at eight-fifteen o'clock

Admit Two   Admission by Invitation

American Humor

Don Antonio, Frank's neighbor's father-in-law, always bragged that he was born in the field, and the earth was his cradle, giving him the ability to grow the biggest and best vegetables. On Sunday morning, as promised, he brought Frank a basket of large tomatoes, beautiful peppers, and zucchinis that would feed a family of four.

"Frank, show me your garden." Frank, having a few days to do some shopping, went to the farm down the road and asked the farmer for the biggest tomatoes, peppers, and eggplants with the stems still intact. Carefully he tied each onto the plants in his garden. Don Antonio stared with his mouth open, almost dropping his Di Nobili cigar and said, "But how could yours be bigger than mine?" Frank continuing with the joke said, "My fertilizer is a family secret." As the old man knelt down and fingered the vegetables, he realized he had been made a fool of.

This he took as a sign of the ultimate disrespect. Frank, not meaning any disrespect, was surprised to see Don Antonio storm out of the garden and quickly return, taking his basket of vegetables. He realized that what he thought was funny here in America, was considered disrespectful to an old world Sicilian man…

Campagna,
Watercolor by Cecelia.

79

Shattered Heart

Yea, though I walk through the valley of death..

Listen up my mind and heart, why am I scared?

It's only bread I need to bring.

Strange, it's November, as a child, the summer home in November, no, only June until September.

Remembering the garden gate, my brother and I swung on laughing, now rusty old and scaly.

Peach tree, my old friend, you look so cold and you've grown old. Will I see you in the spring?

The lush green earth now lays with mounds of ripped up plants.

I hate dusk. The skies steel grey. What will darkness bring today?

This summer house once bright white seems now filled with fright. Why are they here, November, why so late? No lights inside, why do I hesitate. Just open the door and bring in the bread.

With eyes wide, I see uncle holding grandmother's hands.

Both have knarled fingers, transparent skin, veins that look like roots. Once young and strong, now old and frail.

Why so sad? — "Vincenzo is a foolish boy," he says, "Mamma, you soon will die then what will I do?"

1958, this year forced to retire, he no longer has a heart's desire. Carpenters Union Law, 40 years on the job don't count, mandatory retirement is what it's all about.

Squared shouldered, handsome man, clean shaven and always dressed fine, now with a stubble beard, old and bent. This house he built each board, brick and screw he knew.

Never married, would often say, "If wife and mother have a fight, how would I know who is right?" His inward staring eyes must see his life's destiny. I stand spellbound at the mystery of his suffering.

Looking up at me, grandmother says, "*Cara*, (dear) you are a new bride, go home. Your husband waits. We will be fine, thank you for the bread."

Bread, the sustenance of life, my mother would often say. In Sicily,

80

when little and poor she took the inside out of the bread and pretended as if it was olives, beef or cheese."

Sleep that night would not come quick. I pray, tomorrow let it be a better day. Tomorrow came and went and the next day too. Where has my uncle gone? No one knows for sure. His final words, "to Brooklyn I'll go to check on the house and bring back the mail."

He never did return or call.

The priest is here with grave news, they say. "*Signora*, he said, your son is dead. A tragic accident from what I hear." "He fell or jumped it's not quite clear. Yesterday, on the Brooklyn line the speeding train could not stop in time."

A wail and then her anguished cries so loud we all stood still.

Her outstretched hands to the heavens she raised, in them she held, we knew, her shattered heart and first-born son.

On her knees she slowly sank and quietly said, "*Pirchì, Diu miu, Pirchì?*" (why my God, why?)

Dressed all in black in the corner she sat, with lifeless eyes and sobs that shook her. She cried and cried until death took her.

Saturday Before Sundown

As we entered my grandmother's kitchen she was chatting with two friends, one was dabbing her eyes with a handkerchief, holding a picture of "*La Madonna Niura*" (The Black Madonna) in her hand. All I knew was that there is a Sanctuary of The Black Madonna in Tindari, Sicily, overlooking the Tyrrhenian Sea on the north coast. She was known around the world and yet she was held as a mystery, associated with the earth, darkness and most importantly with miracles. Quickly there was a hush and the picture was put away. I had heard that this friend had been diagnosed with the "C" word, as it was referred to in the 1950's. With a wave and a kiss they quietly left.

Saturday was reserved for running errands and preparing for date night. This Saturday was the usual every two months get together of "women only" at grandma's house. Mr. Abraham, the Jewish merchant, would come carrying his two beat up, worn thin with stretched straps and broken buckle suitcases. These were fully packed with bedspreads, curtains, house aprons, and special Italian gold jewelry. We had all received rosary beads made from the petals of real roses which we treasured. They were gifts for christening, communion, and confirmation. The women were able to purchase these items by putting a few dollars down as they continued to pay them off. This was a great way to pay for a trousseau or purchase a new look for your bedroom.

Sicilians were very well educated in the art of haggling. They knew the price of an item as well as the price they could afford. My mother was given inside information as to the psychology of bargaining for large purchases. Especially a suit, overcoat or furniture purchased on Delancey Street. You needed to be the first customer. Merchant and buyer would begin their manipulative behavior. He needed the first sale to make the rest of the day successful and she had limited funds. Or you waited to be the last customer as this too brought success or failure to each. Mr. Abraham had packed up and left. His religion dictated that he be home before sundown and he still had a lot of customers to visit.

My grandmother had already started lunch. Today she would serve "Wonder Food". She poured several blue boxes of *pastina* into the boiling pot. If you had a tooth pulled you would say, "I wonder what to eat, the answer was *pastina*. My belly hurts the answer: "have a little *pastina*." The doctor would suggest that the baby was ready for real food, ah I'll make, and you guessed it. On Saturday, you would also refresh your refrigerator to make room for Sunday's dinner. Out came left over chicken soup, *virdura* (vegetables), *cicoria* and *fasola* (chicory and beans.) Now you could concoct your own special dish of "*pastina* and..." For me it was dressed with olive oil and a little salt and pepper. I don't like cheese. Plain was just fine.

We teenagers now started to ask our mothers "when are we going home so that we could get ready for our dates?" My grandmother took this opportunity to turn the conversation with playful quirkiness to our thoughts about virginity and chaperones. Embarrassed and with red faces we did not answer. She took the lead and began, "In Sicily the chaperones would follow the young lovers and leave enough space for a stolen kiss or two. Older men preferred to marry a young girl because this assured him that she had not had the opportunity to have boyfriends and so he would have the grand pleasure to deflower a virgin. Virginity was regarded as a valuable commodity. If a girl eloped or left with a young man, her disapproving father would reconsider her choice because no one else would want to marry her and he would have to support her. Continuing, the topic changed to the preparing of the bed for the eve of the nuptials by the mother and mother in law, she told us she would be happy to also assist when we married. She continued that the next morning the nuptial blood-spotted bed sheet would be displayed as proof of both consummation of marriage and that the bride was a virgin. Our eyes widened and we listened. To assure that no one would be disappointed mothers often placed a needle in the hem of the girl's bed clothes just in case she needed to prick her finger. She laughed as she said, "If here in America the President wanted a parade of the virgins, for sure if one was sick the other would certainly not march alone." Everyone laughed.

She decided to tell us how she became her daughter's chaperone and the story of the "Loop de Loop".....With hand gestures flying into the air she described her ordeal. Her daughter, our aunt was going out with a wise guy. My description of a wise guy is a man that tries to control his environment and destiny and above all demands and commands respect. He was a tall handsome, young man with devilish blue eyes. For several days he listened to his friends laugh and tease him that he should be careful of the sternness of his new love's mother. After all, she had raised four sons in Sicily while her husband was here in America. He smiled and softly said, "No worries about being chaperoned by her."

As promised, he arrived on Sunday morning ready to take the ladies out for the day, but first he presented flowers to my grandmother saying "*Per voi signora Tumminello*" (for you madam). A sly sideward wink and smile was reserved for my aunt. His charming ways won my grandmother Cecelia over. She remained vigilant to walk between the two love birds. As a widow and having four sons she could not afford anyone's judgmental eye.

He promised them an exciting day. When they arrived at the Loop de Loop (the Cyclone at Coney Island) he gallantly escorted first his new love onto the ride and with a gentlemanly gesture he helped my grandmother sit next to her. Quickly he secured them in and stepped back. He remained off the ride and waited for their return. Upon their return my grandmother's face was the color of red peppers, her voice was hoarse from screaming and her hair was windblown and loose around her shoulders. She said she looked like a *"Scapiddata"* which is a word used for a wanton woman or a vamp with unkempt hair. At the end of the ride, the comb that held her tight bun in place was gone and her scarf was nowhere to be found.

The young man greeted mother and daughter with a big smile and inquired "would you like to go on the ride again?" He also extended an invitation for the following Sunday. My grandmother was fuming and did not speak a word the entire way home.

As she entered her home she immediately knelt before the *Santu Patri.*

She had a small corner shelf that held a framed picture of the Heavenly Father with long white windblown hair and a beard. In front of him was a small, blue glass which held a single wick in the finest olive oil reserved only for him. *"Santu Patri,"* she said "we are in America and so from now on I ask you to be the chaperone and watch over them." "He is a devilish man and you must be observant, *Cui pecura si fa, lu lupu si la mancia* (Whoever behaves as a lamb, is eaten by the wolf). He soon became her son in law and the stories continued. She laughed and laughed as she told us that when Mr. Abraham first saw the picture of the *Santu Patri* he asked if he was her dead grandfather.

We all laughed with no reserve as we heard the story of this usually quiet woman, visualizing her screaming with her hair flying on the roller coaster at Coney Island, doing figure eights seventy five feet above the ground. This was a picture we would not soon forget. We enjoyed the camaraderie and knew that today we had crossed a personal milestone into a very special group, "womanhood." We stood shoulder to shoulder learning from the women we called grandmother, mother, aunt and cousins . . . all this before Sundown on Saturday.

Thanksgiving - New Traditions

Mamma's stance, directing our entire family was that of *"La Capitana,"* the captain. Preparations for the coming holidays began in the summertime. Planted and harvested tomatoes and vegetables would now be transformed. Bottles were filled with cooked sauce. Eggplants were soaked in brine. Hot peppers, roasted, sliced and stuffed with anchovies. The mushrooms we enjoyed were purchased from Mr. Macaluso, the mushroom man, who grew them in a nearby rundown farmhouse. Entering his dark dank basement, the smell of rotting wood, fungus, and wet dirt, forced me to take a step back. I remained there as my parents walked among the raised mushroom beds picking and choosing the best. Soon we thanked the mushroom man and left with two baskets of non-poisonous beauties.

During summer vacation, Frank and I had completed one holiday service. Every morning we helped put five trays of cooked tomatoes, peeled and forced through the food mill, outdoors. The trays were put where the August sun would extract the moisture. Each time we passed, we were reminded to stir the *"Strattu"* in a figure eight motion. With wooden spoon in hand we could not resist a few games of tic tac toe, or draw a funny face. My last recollection was drawing a big heart with a question mark in the middle. Then, one evening, all that remained was enough to be scraped into a deep red gooey ball of *"Strattu-Sicilianu."* Here in America it came in a can and was called tomato paste. Ask any Sicilian lady which tastes better and the response is always, "What are you talking about?" "No comparison." This would be divided and shared with family. *Strattu* would be reconstituted in Sunday sauce, were it gave a rich deep flavor.

During the week we had gone to the Brooklyn Fruit Market and brought back a case of green olives. Today, with the hammer, my job was to whack the olives. As I begin, boing, a few flew in the air; some lost their pits while others lay in two parts. Soon they were perfect and ready to be dressed with garlic, celery, and olive oil at Thanksgiving.

This Thanksgiving was going to be different in that it would be at our house for the first time, only because Mamma relinquished the reigns for this holiday. My mother was planning a traditional Thanksgiving dinner. She consulted the Beautiful Homes magazines for ideas. Her family called her "L'Americana" and this was the perfect holiday for her to start a new tradition. The day came; the house was decorated with honeycomb decorations of Pilgrims, Native Americans, and even place cards. We watched as Mamma curiously ran her hand along the paper tablecloth covered with turkeys as it crinkled to her touch. The centerpiece was a cornucopia filled with autumn flowers. My mother asked my father, "Nick, what do you think?" He looked, paused, and scratched his chin as if he was thinking. "Well," he said, "It's beautiful, but when did we become goats? Are we going to eat the flowers instead of the usual *antipastu*?" He smiled as she lifted her eyes to heaven asking for patience. As she removed the flowers, Mamma replaced them with the *spignola*, an oversized white china platter, with a thread of silver around the edge, *filu di argentu*. This was a wedding gift that she treasured and brought from Castelvetrano. Now it was filled and over-flowing with our past labor. As Mamma lifted her eyes, she noticed our statue of St. Anthony wearing a Pilgrims hat. Oooooh Nooooo!! Poor St. Anthony, even you have become an American! There stood St. Anthony, a hat on his head, with a pumpkin and a turkey at his feet.

As the Pilgrims and Native Americans shared their traditions, so did we. The turkey, *tacchinu*, was proud to share the table with *pulpetti* (meatballs). The mashed sweet potatoes sat next to the stuffed artichokes. Everyone had an input into the menu, and so *vinu russu di casa*, red house wine and golden apple cider filled our glasses. How we would have laughed if I had recited my poem:

Pasqualinu

The fall was approaching; winter was on its way.

Between the two was the dreaded day.

Lu tacchinu named Pasqualinu could think of nothing more,

then keeping the humans away from his door.

When it was time, Pasqualinu played dead

so the humans took his cumpari instead.

The table was surrounded with proud Sicilian-Americans. Glasses raised toasting *La famigghia* and our new Thanksgiving Tradition. BONU PITITTU. . .

Holiday Memory 2012

"Come on, Auntie, hold my arm, I'll help you up the stairs." With a pause and a smile, she says, "It seems like only yesterday Cecelia, I helped you up the stairs."

Elders coming, each bringing their home cooked treasures, still warm, filled bread with salami and cheese rolled and baked the old fashioned way. The special Bundt Cake with drips of white sugar icing, decorated for each special occasion. Young ones bring a special salad made with fruits, nuts and seeds. Don't forget the goat cheese. Another brings the latest wine, tomato that is. Whatever happened to plain red or white?

My children and their loves Christopher, Cheryl and Christina and my grandchildren Nicholas, Karina, Vincent, Ryan, Brandon and Isabella share laughter, a funny joke, embarrassing moment, a shoe flying or a zipper left undone. Now something they can remember. We are all family here, no fear of finger pointing or ridicule.

Pots and pans like cymbals clang. Each one of us takes up a chore. Places set, candles lit, all at one table we sit. Little ones, two on one chair they sit, we stop for a moment to say a prayer.

Now pass the breads, meats and cheese, where is the Tomato Wine, if you please?

Fruits, nuts and sweets galore, and fill my cup with espresso, of course. How fast time goes, the tables clean. Goody bags are packed with promises of "won't eat for a week."

Coats are fetched and shoes are found, mothers search for gifts and toys, don't forget your IPods and Smart phones.

Diaper bags are a thing of the past, now the dogs, CC and Scooter to holiday dinners come. Remember to take their treats and bowls and winter coats.

After the cars pull away and I've waved goodbye, I put my feet up and sigh. Aah, a perfect ending to a perfect day.

"Grazzii a Diu pri la mia famigghia" (Thank you, Lord for my Family).

Grandchildren.

Brother Frank and me.

Men and Women

Often my mother and father would discuss the age old question, "How do men and women differ?"

My mother said "men are like four flags (*quattru banneri*) flapping in the wind, happiness, sadness, passion, and rage." My father agreed. Now my father decided he knew exactly what women were all about. "Women," he said, "are like puppies, they want to be protected, acknowledged, fed, and loved." My mother nodded yes. Both smiled and turned their attention to me.

You see, I was nineteen and about to be married. They continued, "Except when we disagree. Your father goes to fill the car up with gas, and I water my flowers."

Well, after 55 years of marriage to my husband Victor, the car never runs out of gas, and my flowers are always in full bloom.

My Father's Rendezvous

The sun streaming in the kitchen window passing through the colored glass bottles that my mother kept on her windowsill made a pattern that looked like dancing lights. She was preparing lunch dressed in her usual daytime stay-at-home clothes, consisting of a floral housedress, a starched apron, earrings and high heeled shoes. She was always ready for unexpected guests; all she needed to do was remove the apron.

Startled, she looked up at the ceiling, *Rasca, Rasca, ci ci.* She jumped back and pointed at the ceiling saying *"Va rasca li corna di lu diavulu"* (go scratch the devil's horns). *Lu scoiattulu,* the squirrel, was trying to make a nest on the roof. My mother was not a lover of animals. She said to my father: "If that *scoiattulu* sticks his head through the ceiling, *ci dugnu na botta cu la pignata!"* (I'm going to whack it with the pot!).

My father being a man of high energy and determination went out to fix the roof. He climbed the roof and fixed the hole. Hearing him she went out to see what he was doing. He always said *Nsignati l'arti e mettila di parti* (learn the trade and put it aside). Today he would be a roofer, yesterday he was a farmer and tomorrow he may be a shoemaker. As my mother approached, *lu scoiattulu* was jumping toward him. She screamed "Nick, *accura*!" (Watch out!) He lifted his hammer to defend himself, but instead he slipped and plopped on the roof. As he was sliding off the roof, he grabbed a tree limb and landed on the ground.

Quickly, my mother told him to sit down, got him a glass of water and a cold wet cloth for his head. This was a Sicilian cure-all. If you were scared, hurt yourself, or just not feeling well, there you were, doing this three-part ritual. Somehow, it always helped.

A few days later, my mother started to laugh so hard she had tears in her eyes. She said, "Nick, I was thinking of the look of fright on your pale face, and I didn't know if I should catch you or get the camera."

Since retiring, my father enjoyed working in his vegetable garden and taking an afternoon nap under the grape arbor. The arbor, made up of wooden slats, was covered with red grapes on one side and black grapes on the other. Everyone enjoyed picking them and eating them as they ripened.

As soon as lunch was over, Mommy busied herself with woman's work. She often said *"Signuri vi ringraziu ca Nick avi stu giardinu, sinnò*

l'avissi sempri ntra li pedi. (Thank you God that Nick has this garden or else he would be always under my feet). She knew he would soon bring in the mature vegetables.

As Catholics, we never ate meat on Fridays, so for dinner she was going to make *suppa di cucuzza e pumadoru, basilicò e ova.* (Squash soup made with tomato, basil, and eggs).

After he weeded and watered and brought the vegetables to my mother, he sat in his lounge chair under the arbor which was large enough to cover a table and chairs. The lush grapes and leaves made a cool covering on this hot August day.

What none of us knew was that he was having an afternoon rendezvous *cu lu scoiattulu* (the squirrel).

He later described this beautiful *scoiattulu* with black fur and a stiff bushy tail like the plume on the mounted policeman's hat from the old country, with white bristles, *(lu pilu niuru cu la cuda tisa comu la piuma di lu carabineri supra lu cavaddu)* and wise expressive eyes (*occhi furbi*) that watched his every move.

He started with three *scoiattuli,* but two of them soon lost interest.

Only this one came back. Patiently, day in and day out, he tried to get the squirrel to eat from his hand. Closer and closer the *scoiattulu* came and on this day the *scoiattulu* jumped on his shoulder and ate peanuts from his hand.

Hearing my mother starting to sweep behind him, he called her "Jennie, Jennie, *Veni talìa, talìa"* (look, look) in a hushed voice.

She turned around only to see *lu scoiattulu* on his shoulder. Thinking he was going to attack him again, she quickly hit him with the broom. Whack! Plop! Oh! *Madonna mia, chi ci facisti?* (Mother Mary what have you done?) They both stood speechless looking at the dead squirrel.

To their surprise, regaining his strength and limping quickly he ran up a tree.

My father, looking at my mother whose eyes were wide with fright, said *"Poviru Pippineddu,* after two months of feeding him, he finally trusted me and now all he can say is don't trust the man with peanuts, and watch out for the crazy lady with the broom!"

Winter came and the story was retold many times. Bringing laughter to friends and relatives, especially when my father said he never saw my mother speechless before and her eyes looked like they had seen a ghost.

Soon, summer came and we were all invited to meet his new friend Giorgiu, *lu scoiattulu.*

We all looked around; there was not a broom in sight.

Four Legged Treasure

Our throw-away society allows us to say – it's just a table, a lamp or another human being that has no worth, I matter and nothing else. The moment we say we have a favorite thing, that possession becomes part of our history.

When I look at the table I love, it becomes a moving picture show, with my father as the main character. A young boy of 7 or 8 in Sicily that was an apprentice to a blacksmith, long hours and heavy work shoeing horses, making wagon wheels, he hammered and forged iron into reality. *Batti lu ferru mentri è caudu*, strike while the iron is hot. No longer was he sheltered and surrounded with only familiar village dialects and customs. He learned from the travelers that were seeking enlightenment and answers to their existence and that of the universe. Curiosity and seeking knowledge became part of his nature.

America offered him a job in the wrought iron field. He designed and made furniture for the rich of Spain and Portugal. The table he brought home was a culmination of many techniques, both old world and new, he called it art. With a black marble top, one inch thick, and two arm lengths long, it sits on legs that are caressed with strength and stamina into a curvaceous bend and curl. With appliqués of long leaves pressed and formed and the most beautiful bouquet of iron flowers at the center of the base. The shine of the marble mirrored many images of its extraction from a far away quarry.

It held center stage in our living room until television came to our home. A clear view of the T.V. became the number one priority. Placed in the entry foyer, it held a vase filled with handmade paper roses. Moving to Queens, it happily sat with live plants and climbing ivy in the porch.

With the passing of my parents, it became mine. Proudly, it holds family pictures of the past and always room for new additions. Now, estimated age 80 years young, with the warmest living heart and soul it is forever a picture show.

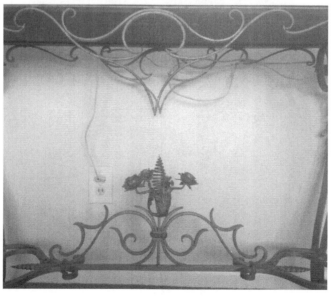

Sound of Life 1963

Chilled vessels filled with golden liquid stood like sentinels anticipating the celebration.

As the clock on the mantel bonged, the two hands of time that rested upon each other began to move apart.

The vessel filled with life began to stir. Bubbles beginning to crash into each other, the effervescence like a concerto rising toward the cork. Each burst of bubbles carried an urgency to be released.

What was to be a quiet and restful night was now a forced exit onto the frozen landscape. Horn blowing, no one in sight, vision blurred by the storm, we arrived. Chaos swirled around us, lights glaring, faceless voices loud and demanding. No time for reasoning, the cork of life, ready to pop.

Pop! The cork flew to the heavens smashing the stars, creating heavenly fireworks that showered the earth with the most beautiful cry of new life.

"Felici Annu Novu, Cecelia, a vostra picciridda è bedda."

"Happy New Year Cecelia, your baby girl is beautiful."

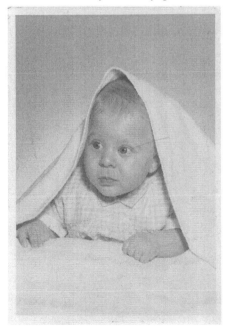

Only a Day Dream

The shrilling alarm clock showed 6 am. Eyes opened and taking a deep breath, I placed my feet hesitantly on the floor. I gave the soft bed a longing glance and wondered what adventure today would bring.

As a young woman, I was chief cook and bottle washer to a husband, four children, Poochie, Fluffy, and a fish tank on my kitchen counter filled with guppies that flitted from side to side waiting to be fed. My Phone was ringing, T.V. blasting, children having – let's call them- loud discussions in the living room.

The endless questions began. "What time are we going into the pool?" "Two o'clock" I said. "Where is my shoe?" "There, the dog has it." "Do I have to wear a tie to Suzy's wedding?" "Yes, and your blue suit too." "How many teeth do I have?" "Let's count them, one, two, and three."

The clock bonged two and there stood Lori-Ann with the towels, Billy with a jug of green citrus juice that they called bug juice, Carolyn with the pan filled with popcorn and Christopher with a handful of pennies to toss into the air and then dive into the pool for them.

I picked up my overflowing basket of clothing that needed to be folded, then out the back door onto the covered porch, and there was the pool.

Through the laughing and splashing I heard chirping. Shh, listen! At the end of the garage, my father had built and hung a birdhouse. There they were little beaks open and waiting for Mama to feed them. She swooped in with her beautiful red breast, standing on the perch with spindly legs, fed them worms, looked around and repeated this ritual over and over. I was mesmerized.

As she took flight, I noticed the dark shadow of her outstretched wings on the lawn. She ascended to the heavens. I followed.

Feeling peace and weightlessness, I soared above the billowy clouds and light blue sky. The trees were covered in a multitude of green hues that I had never seen. We flew, ever so mindful, in our hearts of the unconditional love and care our babies needed until they too could fly.

"Mommy, Mommy, the phone is ringing!" Returning to earth like a ball being sucked into a tube, I reached for the phone. "Hi," my husband said, "Where did you all go? I called before but no one answered."

As the grandfather clock bonged three, to my husband I said, "I don't know, I really don't know." Hanging up the phone, I continued to hum *Volare*, "*E volavo, volavo felice più in alto del sole ed ancora più su,*" and I flew, I flew happily to the heights of the sun. This song was inspired by two of Marc Chagall's paintings…. "*Le coq rouge*" and "*Le peintre et la modella.*"

Age Does Matter

It was April 27th, a beautiful sunny day, my birthday. Looking in the big mirror over the fireplace, I combed my long blonde hair into the usual ponytail.

My ponytail hairdo was a carefree style. Victor and I looked contented in our 1957 powder blue convertible, top down, coming from the pool or just having fun as newlyweds.

Newlyweds, young and carefree, it seemed for just a moment and then, it was 1962. Now we were driving a brown four door Oldsmobile, definitely an "old man's car," but safety and space was what we needed. I was 25 years old and married for 5 years. Vic and I had just become homeowners. The price of the house was $17,100, with a $3,000 down payment. Our mortgage, taxes and insurance would come to $71.00 per month.

As a stay at home mom to Lori-Ann, Billy and Carolyn, 3 children under 3 years old, Vic's salary of $75.00 a week was all we had. He said, "You know, as homeowners, this means we have to tighten our belts," three little words that I hated for many years. "But don't worry", he said, "If we budget our expenses to 4 paydays a month, we can buy all the extras we want with the 5th paycheck. $75.00 times 4 gave us $300 extra a year."

As I continued to stand in front of the mirror, I could see the growing responsibility of our family needing more and we as parents being happy with less. Taking the $7.00 for a haircut was a big bite out of our budget, but if I was going to be an adult, then my ponytail had to go, and it did. One snip of the hairdresser's scissors transported me into the grown-up world.

Age 25, a birthday I will never forget, my ponytail gone, my family complete.

And then…Little did I know 10 years later, Christopher, baby #4 came along and the story continued…. "Children are the cane of your old age." (*I figghi sunnu lu bastuni di la vicchizza.*)

The Tie

At a time of sorrow, it's human nature to do something out of the ordinary.

My mother never liked the color black. She always said, "When I die the grandchildren should not be made sadder by what they wear. I want to see red, my favorite color." Abiding by her wishes all the floral arrangements from the Gates of Heaven to the Bleeding Heart to the six baskets from the grandchildren surrounded her with red flowers.

As I stood there looking at my mother, my mind had this profound thought, "she's just sleeping, how peaceful she looks." What silliness at a time when your inner child felt like screaming and kicking and say I want my mommy, you find the strength to refrain from hysterics. It's the grown-up thing to do.

People come up to you and praise your loved one with tears in their eyes. They leave you with the feeling of an arm around your shoulder and a warm embrace. Her best friend tells me of the time she was at a Bronx Sanitarium, gravely ill, so despondent and lonely that she closed her eyes and prayed for death. As her eyes fluttered open, she saw what she thought was the Madonna. My mother was standing in the doorway in a blue dress, the rays of the sun on her and the bouquet of flowers was an image she will never forget. With many blessings to our family, she walked away.

My brother Frank walked to the coffin knelt down and said his private prayers to our mother. The silence of the room was broken by a gasp and the murmur of the old women as they clutched at their hearts and fingered their rosary beads. Frank's *cravatta russa* (red tie), was the cause.

La signura Josephina got up and approached Frank; she was always the outspoken one.

My mother's physical being left this earth but her smile, good humor, and loving heart remained. I could hear her saying, *"La signura, in invernu e stati sempri avi castagni p'arrustiri."* (In winter and summer she always has chestnuts to roast. My mothers' translation, the busybody always has something to say.

Looking over at my brother I could see his face getting paler and his ears getting redder. As I approached, *La signura* was pointing her finger saying, "I will buy you a respectful tie." Frank tried to explain that his red tie was worn to show respect for his mother, but *La signura* persisted. Quietly, he said, "If you would change places with my mother, I will wear a tie that would please you." The last word was not out of his mouth before she scurried away like a mouse being chased by a cat.

Frank looked at me puzzled, as he said, "I am good and I am kind, but don't step on my eyes" (*sugnu bonu e caru, ma nun mi pistari l'occhi*). This proverb was used ONLY at a time when in the blink of an eye your patience and self control was lost.

And, as for *La signura*, she went elsewhere to roast her chestnuts.

The Seeds of Destiny-1984

An ideal way to start the day would be to hear the trill and twittering of song birds. If you happen to be asleep at nine o'clock on any given day during the summer months, you would be awakened by the corn husk broom that was wielded by Mamma. Bing, bam, boom against the iron rungs of the *branda* (cot), which I was sleeping on. Housekeeping needed to be finished before she went out. This was such a morning. She was an early riser and probably woke the rooster up. "Mamma, where are we going today, it's raining out!" "Oh", she said, "So now you're a sugar dolly (*pupidda di zuccaru*)? We need to go to the post office." The conversation ended and soon we were on our way. The clouds were scattering as we walked arm in arm with a twirling umbrella. Francis Lewis Boulevard was still a country road, without sidewalks or curbs. It made avoiding the puddles an adventure. The fifteen or so blocks to town became a time for a story to be told.

Pointing to a house or land, my grandmother would say, "See this vacant lot? When you were little, it was filled with dandelions; we called them *denti di liuni*, (teeth of a lion) because of their jagged leaves. The Americans called them weeds. We called them *insalata* (salad)." Next we came to the mushroom man's house and the egg lady's house. With a sad look, she told me about the beautiful property my parents had to relinquish to the bank for back taxes. The Great Depression forced its return. They were going to build a small summer house on Long Island with the intention of eventually making it into a year-round home. Instead, they opted for a home for us in the Bushwick section of Brooklyn, where we would learn to be more Americanized.

We went to school with children that only spoke English. My mother wanted us to be completely immersed in the American ways. We were to judge people for whom they were and not focus on where they came from. Mamma continued, "I love property and if allowed by finances I would own it all." She recounted the story of the man she had loaned five hundred dollars to. Because of his dishonesty, she lost the opportunity to purchase one piece of property. Soon, a more desirable piece became available. Mr. Kenneth made sure that she was able to buy it.

We heard the clang, clang of the railroad signal, gates coming down and the tooting of the train pulling into the Rosedale Station.

Realizing we had arrived in town, we crossed the street to the Post Office. The sun was shining brightly as we walked. A man with a seersucker suit and a straw hat in his hand approached us. Mamma got the giggles as he shook her hand. They shared a few pleasantries and shaking my hand, he left.

"Mamma, who is he?"

"Ah, he is Mr. Kenneth, the real estate man. Do you see all of these stores, the funeral parlor, the candy store, the post office, and his real estate office which is also a travel agency and insurance company? They are all his. He knows all the available properties."

Raising her eyes to the sky and with a sudden sideways glance, as though she had looked into the future, she said, "Wait, why can't you become a real estate lady when you grow up? You would be well respected and best of all; you would be able to buy property."

"Oh Mamma, we'll see."

At the age of twelve, destiny had a lot of work to do. The idea remained and always intrigued me. Her one piece of advice was, "*L'occhiu di lu patruni ingrossa la crapettu,* (the eye of the owner fattens the goat.) When in business, you must always be present."

Years passed, and then as a wife and a mother of four I went to adult education classes in the evening. I decided that I would learn something new every six months. My father was a great believer of, "If you do the same thing over and over, what exactly are you learning?" The classes were interesting, from Karate to Knitting to Magic to Gourmet Cooking. They taught us to cook *pasta con piselli,* when did this become gourmet? Pasta and peas, scrumptious when made with fresh shelled peas was usually served on Wednesday during Lent. This gave me a chuckle, thinking if I served this dish to company they would probably leave some money under the scarf on my dresser wondering if I had fallen on hard times. The classes that now interested me were geared towards going back to work. I had enjoyed being a stay-at-home wife and mother for twenty plus years. A Real Estate Sales Person course was being offered and I signed up. The year was Nineteen Hundred Eighty Four. My mother always said, "When you put your shoes on to go to work, try to make it worth your while."

A few part time jobs later, a School Crossing Guard, a Greeting Card Merchandiser, and even an Alexander's Department store floater. I never knew which department I would be in until I got to work. These were all stepping stones to re-entering the work force. Diversification was something I enjoyed. At age fifty plus years old, I went to Nassau Community College to become a Real Estate Broker and then a Mortgage Broker and soon a Commissioner of Deeds. My classes were also in Early Childhood Development. As a child, being a Kindergarten Teacher was also interesting. First comes love then comes marriage and soon came a baby carriage. And so becoming a paid teacher was not to be. With my children and some of the neighbor's children, I enjoyed teaching at my home's "Ding Dong School," where I learned and grew along with the children. Real Estate was my destiny and so it became a reality. My office, Cecelia Realty Corporation, was in Rosedale, Queens not far from Mr. Kenneth. Real Estate is still one of my loves.

Recently there was an opportunity to become an apprentice to a Tattoo Artist at Wyld Chyld Tattoo and so I am licensed to body pierce and tattoo. As a hobby, I enjoy watercolor art, it has innocence and clarity.

Life has so many twists and turns that if we keep turning corners, we never know what we can become. It's fun to see how destiny unfolds into reality. If you are reading my book, I can add Published Author to my list of accomplishments. Wow! My most exciting and biggest surprise yet! Share my motto, "Life is too serious to be taken seriously. If there is something you want to do – or be – do it now." Remember—"WHAT IS A SUN DIAL IN THE SHADE?".....

Don't Worry! Be Happy!

"*Sugnu fissa e cuntenta*," my grandmother always said, "sometimes it's fun to be foolish and happy." You realize you are being made a fool of or perhaps you look foolish but it is a feeling of sheer merriment for your soul to enjoy the moment. We sometimes get so serious that if a smile creeps up from our childhood we shake it off and assume our adult persona. Well, this doesn't happen to me that often, if there is something to laugh about, I do welcome and enjoy the opportunity. And so the following stories are just too share a simple pleasure.

When little, I asked my mother "Why do I have to learn to clean? My mother answered, "Well, when you become a princess how will know if your servants are doing a good job of keeping your castle clean?" With this in mind I continued to put lemon oil on that gauzy rag we called cheese cloth and polished all the wood in sight.

Making meatballs was an adventure, first you had to overcome the feel of cold raw meat that had been mixed in a bowl with eggs, cheese, parsley, and a few tablespoons of sauce to make them juicy, oh I forgot the fresh breadcrumbs made from the stale bread grated on the cheese grater. Now let's make the golf ball size meatballs. As I rolled the meatball, some had raisins, others didn't. Mom reminded me to put a thumbprint in the middle. Why Mom? "Oh, that's necessary to be able to tell the ones you made." With a sideward glance and a knowing smile, we continued. You do know it is so the middle of the meatball cooks as evenly as the outside, so I was told.

Studying for a test, the night would end and it would be past my bedtime, so my mother would assure me that if I put the book under my pillow I would absorb all the knowledge needed. Looking for a reason to abandon my books, I happily agreed.

The time had come to reinvent myself. The wardrobe of slacks and blouses topped with a jacket was my normal dress. I decided that in the Leap Year of 1988 I wanted to look more modern while going back to college. What were the young people wearing? Taking myself to Gertz Department Store in Jamaica, I began with the boutique department. I choose several garments and entered the dressing room. My first choice was a dress I thought quite stylish and different from what was hanging in my closet. As I put it on, I noticed that I resembled the familiar toilet paper caddy with the doll face and a very, very poufy skirt whose job it was to cover the next roll of toilet paper. Quickly it came off and went back on the hanger.

Onto the next dress, this was a lovely brown dress with gold chains on the bodice. As I squirmed into the dress I looked in the mirror only to burst out laughing with an expression of glazed disbelief on my face. My panty girdle was longer than the mini dress. As the saleswoman entered we both began to laugh. All the while the popular songs of 1988 played in the background, one was "Every Rose Has a Thorn" and "Red Red Wine," but the best was, "Don't Worry! Be Happy!" Soon I left the store with a lovely brown dress, a new panty girdle, and a big, big, happy smile. . . *Fissa e cuntenta.*

Always the Same Song-1999

Why is he walking towards me? Who is he? Why is he calling me a Sigi? What is a Sigi? Unbelievable, a grown man with bloodshot eyes and slurred speech, anger on his face, and it's all directed at me. "So you're the Sicilian I heard about? Where do your people come from?" Speechless for a moment, but taught to respect elders, even if they were inebriated, I responded, "My mother comes from Castelvetrano, and my father comes from Mazzara Del Vallo." The words Mazzara Del Vallo didn't leave my mouth before he became a wildman. His glass of wine spilled and his face contorted. I had become fodder for his rage. "No, I don't carry a switch blade and my family is not connected." Thinking, the only thing my father was connected to was the alarm clock. He left at sunrise and returned after the sun went down. Looking towards my friend and her family, I was astonished, they stood silent. They accepted his behavior without challenge.

This was to be my friend's fifteenth birthday party. We were in the same class and I had been asked to dinner. As "He" continued bombarding me with questions, my parents' voices came into my head: "Always be proud to be called a Sicilian, no one on this earth has the right to make you feel bad, not young or old. Stand tall and know that you come from a family that has never eaten off of the shoulders of others. The person in front of you represents himself and ideas that he has absorbed from others. Make no excuse for him and know he stands in his own stink." Never had I been involved in this type of discrimination.

Thinking back, I could see my father being drawn into the dance of the two roosters. Men from the North of Italy would start with the insinuation that Southerners were uneducated and not as refined as the Northerners, that his town produced many men of questionable character. They would begin; one word and then two. The conversation would include a few barbed innuendos. My father would end it quickly with his one sentence, "*Ma pirchì sempri la stissa canzuna?*" (But why always the same song?) With a pat on the back, a promise of a toast to good health and the conversation was redirected to planting, new cars, and social clubs. Countrymen from surrounding towns in Sicily also riled each other up. My father reminded them that saints are in heaven and as long as there is greed, there will be corruption. It didn't matter if they wore a white collar, blue collar, or a round collar.

From time to time the old Northern and Southern dragon reared its ugly head, like ashes that smolder and reignite.

The year was now Nineteen Hundred and Ninety-Nine. With it came the opportunity for a long dreamed of vacation to Rome, Venice and Florence. Venice was picturesque, with gondolas, water taxis and a flooded and still spectacular St. Mark's Square. The buildings, old and decaying were now partially covered with new brick. As I placed my hands and cheek on the old stone-work, there was a sense of time standing still. Florence, with its magnificent churches, ancient ruins and lush countryside was an artists' dream. In the evening we walked the streets of Rome and marveled at The Trevi Fountain. Following tradition, we tossed in our coins so that we may return again. The art works by the famous painter Caravaggio were breathtaking. The Pantheon, so mathematically perfect, that Michelangelo said, "It was designed by the angels." Giovanni Bernini's "Pulcino della Minerva" and Christ the Redeemer by Michelangelo were sensational images for the eyes. We enjoyed Rome, this museum without walls. Statuary was everywhere. The leaning Tower of Pisa was being repaired, on a tilt for eight hundred years, was it an architectural miscalculation or a natural inclination?

Our tour guide announced that we would take an unscheduled, brief side trip to view the Imperial Roman Coliseum. Hearing stories and having seen glossy pictures of this magnificent piece of architecture, I was excited. To imagine the deafening noise of the audience as they watched the Christians and the beasts, water sports, and chariot races. Fifty thousand spectators listening to the blaring trumpets, beating of the drums and the gladiators shouts – "*Ave Cesare, morituri te salutant*" (Hail Cesar, those who are about to die salute you.)

Exiting the bus, I noticed a young man dressed as a gladiator from sandals to spear, asking tourists to take a picture with him for five dollars. How industrious I thought, until he approached a group of intellectually disabled young adults that had shared our bus. He was finger pointing in a most harassing way and asking for ten dollars to take a picture. Witnessing this injustice, I decided to side-step my group. Approaching this young man, I told him in Sicilian to "Go away and take a walk" (*vattinni, va fatti na caminata*). He questioned on where my people came from. My daughter responded, and there it was, his contorted face at his hearing Mazzara Del Vallo. One word led to another and I was drawn into the dance of the two roosters. As we continued, the tour guide returned and said, "Quickly, quickly Cecelia, back on the bus!" There I stood wondering,

"Cu è lu babbu? Lu babbu è iddu o cu ci va appressu?" (Who is the fool, the fool, or the one that follows him?)

As for my photo with the Coliseum in the background, perhaps I will do what our Sicilian ancestors did. I will find a photographer with a trompe l'oeil backdrop drenched with symbolism; mine will be of the elusive Coliseum. ARRIVEDERCI ROMA …..

Note: Mazzara Del Vallo after World War ll became Mazara Del Vallo.

Deafening Sound of Silence -2001

We had come to see if all was well at the country home after the hurricane of 1954. Trees that had stood strong and tall were now uprooted by the wind and rain. My brother, father and I stood and marveled at how in calm weather, you would never imagine this to happen.

My father became pensive, with head down as though looking into a reflective pool at the thought of his own mortality. He remembered these trees as saplings being planted and nurtured by him and Mamma. The one that saddened him the most was our magnificent fig tree. Every fall we would tie each outstretched branch together, lovingly covered with mats made from swamp reeds and the final tar paper wrapping to protect it from the harsh winter. It was then ready to be crowned with an old soup pot or wash basin. The earth had been nourished all summer with a compost made from vegetable peelings, grass cuttings and fish heads. Looking around he said, "how quickly life changes."

He began to tell us about how as a boy in Sicily, he was always attentive to the traveling scholars, astrologers and the astronomers. They told stories of the prophecies, predictions and interpretations of Nostradamus who was a celebrated physician and soothsayer. He used occult sciences to predict the future. Looking at the two of us, my father said that the one prediction he wished he could see if true was that the world would end as we know it. This was to happen before the end of the year 2000. He said, "You children have a chance to see what happens, but for sure I will not."

Years came and years went into the great abyss. It was now the end of the year 2000. My brother and I raised our glass and our eyes to heaven and toasted my father, assuring him that the world was still here. The year 2001 was well underway, when the unimaginable happened.

Neither advanced scientific knowledge nor large amounts of money could have changed the events of this day. September 11, 2001, a day we will never forget.

That morning, when the phone rang, my husband Victor and I were anticipating a call from my son Christopher and daughter-in-law Cheryl announcing the birth of our fifth grandchild. Instead, the call was from my daughter Lori-Ann, "We've been attacked" she said "Turn on the news; a plane just hit the Twin Towers!" Turning on the television,

Victor and I remained transfixed on what we saw. A few days before, on a New York holiday we had visited the top of the Twin Towers with the grandchildren. Why? And how could this have happened here in New York? Soon we were on alert. The chain of events began.

My son Christopher lived in Middle Village, across the street from Juniper Valley Park, which had a clear view of the New York City Skyline and watched as the first plane hit the tower. He immediately called my daughter Carolyn who worked on 57th Street and shouted into the phone, "Get out of the city!" She met up with my son-in-law Chris and together they sprinted across the 59th Street Bridge, not knowing what may happen, trying to get as far away and quickly as possible. We were unable to call or find out what was going on until they arrived home late that night.

Living minutes from Kennedy Airport, all we heard were the sirens of emergency vehicles responding to this tragedy. The sky became a dead zone. The usual roar of the planes ceased. People were walking zombie-like, with hollow eyes. I sat on my front steps, hugging my knees like a child not knowing, what next? *Nel nome del Padre, e del Figlio e dello Spirito Santo…Gesù* (making the sign of the cross.) Name of the Father, the Son and the Holy Spirit, Jesus, I began to pray like a child in Sicilian, promising to give something in the hopes of my children's safe return. My son Billy called from Long Island and soon arrived.

The days that followed were filled with stories of those that did not return. A young woman we knew perished. Her father went to the site everyday with her picture in the hopes that someone had seen her. He searched and searched refusing to clean his ash covered shoes in fear that it may be his daughter's ashes that clung to them. After many months, a wallet and purse belonging to a family member were returned by authorities, thinking she too had perished. Thankfully, she had left her office, with money in hand to get coffee across the street when the plane hit her building. To this day, her ash covered suit remains stored away in her closet.

We sometimes pretend to have forgotten, but we never will. My father's words came crashing into my thoughts. Our world as we knew it did end that day. How quickly life changes. . .

Ah! Sicilia Bedda 2009

Was it the earth shaking under my feet or was it my knees? The anticipation had now become reality. Childhood stories swirled in my mind. Feast for the senses was repeated by all that came from Sicily. I am a great believer in the proverb *"Quannu lu piru è fattu, cari sulu,"* When the pear is ripe it will fall by itself. And it did. It took me until June, 2009 to arrive in Sicily. My spirit soared at the thought that I stood on the largest island, Sicily, in the Mediterranean Sea. It was the motherland of my parents and grandparents.

My daughter Carolyn and I joined the 15th annual Sicily tour with Arba Sicula/Sicilian Dawn. It is an international organization that promotes the language and culture of Sicily, led by Professor Gaetano Cipolla. His vast knowledge of Sicily brought us to places that felt intimate and others that allowed us to see for ourselves the influences of the original Italic people, Greeks, Romans, Byzantines, Saracens, Spaniards, French and so many more. Visiting the Temple of Segesta we noticed the golden stone columns, some fluted, some not. Were they tumbled in anger or merely abandoned? The earth beneath my feet felt as though it had been trampled on by so many, it was parched and crumbling. Vision and memory blurred as we continued viewing churches. The craftsmanship of the church's exteriors and their interior altars was dizzying. How much time and talent was used to bring about such beauty. At the Mandralisca Museum we saw a valuable Renaissance painting prior to a general viewing. In Noto, the Baroque architecture of the balconies was impressive. Il Teatro Greco's open air production of *Edipo in Colono* with live actors and animals at the foot of Mt. Etna whose ash was rising to heaven is my fondest memory. We enjoyed grand dinners and simple pizza. In Sicilian cuisine the many influences are very conspicuous from their pastries to the pasta sauces.

Sicily will forever be mentally, emotionally, and physically entrenched in my soul. With twenty-four wonderfully charming strangers we began our adventure. I went to Sicily without any expectations. My father loved America, but would say he still heard the "Siren of the Sea" calling all the Sicilians home. Many left the island for better economic times. They took their *"Dono di Dio,"* (gift from God) with them. Stone cutters, artist and fine craftsmen left with their talents as they assimilated into their new countries. If Sicily could talk, it would say, *"Prima t'insignu e poi ti perdu,"* first I teach you and then I lose you.

Each day was exhilarating and nostalgic. We had traveled from New York to Rome and then to Palermo where we began our days of travel. Sicily was as if I was looking at life through a kaleidoscope, it was always changing... Again I say, *"Ah! Sicilia Bedda."*

Human Heart

Your eyes see all the external beauty of Sicily. But the heart of a Sicilian is filled with the human element above all. Upon seeing the ladies in Palermo, June 2009, my thoughts were filled of mother, grandmother, aunts and all the ladies that have influenced me. How many stories they could tell!

As with spring you listen for a bird's song.

Summer the first mosquito bite.

Fall the colorful leaves gently falling.

And winter that brings a white clean cover and hush to all…

Fifty Five Years of Marriage - 2012

The question is asked: "Where did you meet Poppy," my grandchildren wanted to know? "Well, you see, Poppy picked me up at the beach." You look over and they all have a quizzical look. "Why would he pick you up? Did you fall?" "No, that was what it was called in the good old days of 1954. When a boy meets a girl and he is interested in dating her, he would pick her up and get her phone number."

"It was the end of June. My friend and I decided we would be graduating soon and so we wanted to play hooky from school for the first time. We took the bus to the beach at Rockaway Playland. The next day we planned to go to the Paramount Theater to see a Rock and Roll Show. Poppy and his friend decided to go to the beach instead of work that day too. When young ladies packed their beach bag it included an extra fried veal cutlet sandwich just in case a special boy came by. A red plaid thermos was filled with ice tea made from tea leaves and cooled, a nice blanket, portable radio and suntan lotion. The radio was always tuned to Rock and Roll." Looking at my two granddaughters, I said, "Boys were the hunters, they would roam the beach until they saw someone they liked. Remember, a boy will chase you, until you catch him."

"We girls would bat our eyelashes. No, no, not with a real bat, it means we would flutter our eyelashes and get flirty," I explained to my four grandsons. The boys would ask what neighborhood we came from. At this, my husband said "Remember guys, the first thing you want to know is how far I have to travel if I take her out." "That day Poppy asked me for a date and his friend asked my friend out." At this point my husband was asked, "Why did you like Grammy best?" His reply, "Well, it was a windy day and all I could see was her long blond hair flying. Besides, she made a wicked veal cutlet sandwich and she was cute." They all made kissing sounds and swooned. I continued that we went into the ocean, waves were way over my head and I told poppy I couldn't swim, he said not to worry, take my hand I won't let anything happen to you.

Again kissing and swooning sounds and added, "Oh how romantic!" We dated for one year and Poppy bought me an engagement ring and soon we planned to marry. A million and one preparations were made. The music would be more of the serious nature with some Sicilian music, but defiantly not the silly Mexican Hat Dance or the silly Bunny

Hop. We decided that we would have a classy, catered affair and not the usual beer and sandwich wedding. The price for this sit down dinner was seven dollars and fifty cents per person and it included the flaming jubilee. The waiters would carry bowls of cherries with liquor that was set aflame. It would be drizzled over vanilla ice cream. It looked dramatic with the lights off.

The night before the wedding I put a few 1957 pennies and the St. Joseph statue on the window sill. This was the Sicilian guarantee for sunshine and *buona fortuna*. On our wedding day, when I got up, it was raining. Not convinced that the Sicilian proverb "*Sposa bagnata è sposa fortunata*" (a wet bride is a happy bride), I said a little prayer and decided to sleep longer.

As is the custom, the dining room table was set with a beautiful cloth, liqueur glasses were in place and the large tray of cookies with *confetti* was ready for the guest that came to the church. They would come back to the house afterwards. Before the wedding, the close relatives came to the house to see me dressed and wish my happiness as I left for St, Clare's Church. I would now be leaving my parents' home and returning as a married woman with my husband. My husband added to the story. "Have you kids seen the picture of the big church clock that says your grandmother was late to the wedding?" I could not blame the rain because the sun was out big and bright. Late or not we were married and happy. The reception was next and as we entered, the band leader announced our names. We looked around because he had our names wrong. Slight correction by my brother and we were now Mr. and Mrs. The music started and they played songs that we didn't pick. Correction was not necessary since we all enjoyed the Bunny Hop and the Mexican Hat Dance was a smash. The honeymoon, our *viaggiu di nozzi* was in Pennsylvania. We got married on April 28, 1957 a day after my twentieth birthday. Now this special place in Pennsylvania known for honeymooners was... Well, let's just say the brochures were great. The place was not what we expected.

The weather was too cold for the pool and the ski slope was mud. We followed hiking signs that said we would find a bat cage. Aah, finally something interesting. As we got close there it was, a real hanging baseball bat in a cage. The whole thing was so bizarre that we just laughed. We must have been in love because here we were laughing about it and saying that one day we would tell and laugh with our grandchildren. The big attractions at night, going under the limbo stick with other honeymooners, shooting pool and the rifle range. But wait, there is more. We went home

Jimmy - Lena - Lorenzo - Anna -Dad - Mom - Mamma - Frank
Cecelia & Victor

Grandchildren - strong Sicilian traits - Loyalty - Humor - Artistic Vision.

on the Greyhound bus to our apartment which was one house away from your great grandmother and upstairs from Aunt Annie and Uncle Lorenzo. The following day we went to my parents' house so we could open the wedding envelopes.

At the wedding, Mamma, your great-great grandmother held "*la burza*," the big satin bag with the fancy lace and a draw string on top stuffed with the money gifts. This she held between her knees for safe keeping. Now, you can be assured that there is no robber that would have been able to steal anything. It's important that as you open the envelopes you must make a note of what each person gave you. This is necessary so that you will not make "*la mala figura*," a bad show when it comes time to return equal or more to their family member. "Mom," I asked, "how did everyone like the wedding?" She said, "Everyone loved the music and the food was great, even Aunt So and So said that everything was spectacular, except, her second cup of coffee was not as burning hot as the first. We all had a great big belly laugh and so Poppy and I decided that we would make this our "marriage vow for happiness." If the only thing in our life to be judged is the second cup of hot coffee, we would know that things in our life together were just fine. And they are. My children have heard this many times. Hopefully it has taken some of their stress away. Now I prayed that my grandchildren would realize you can't make everyone happy and that they too would share in, "Our Big Secret to Happiness." "*L'amuri nun è bellu si nun c'è stuzzicarellu,*" Love is not beautiful unless you can both tease and be stimulating.

120

In the Blink of an Eye 2012

The day begins:
a spot of water
one foot wet
and then another.
Safe and orderly is my home.
The water is here,
the water is there,
Oh my, it's everywhere.
Rains are falling,
the basement's flooding.
Mom, Mom, what can we do?
Expensive candy, toys and gifts
water covered through and through.
What waste, what waste!
Treasures gathered over years
now destroyed.
What do I rescue?
Family photos with faces blurred,
linens too fine to use, I saved,
submerged and destroyed, I stand numb.

Why do we save?
Why do we treasure?

Blink your eye, it's gone forever.
The water's now decreasing;
the pile of ruined treasures is increasing.
I vow, "Nothing is too fine to use."

Nothing is safe and must be saved.
Let's use them all.

Enjoy, enjoy, and not save,
and call them what they really are:
nothing but leftovers.

As Sicilians say "MINESTRA RIQUARIATA" (It's
nothing more than old reheated soup)

Super Storm Aftermath 2012

Was it an act of God, a freak of nature or the devil blowing off steam? In the olden days the prophets would roam the earth telling of the impending doom, today a simple push of a button and television will put us all on the edge of disaster. The waters will rise; the wind will gust at alarming speeds; make plans to evacuate. As I prepared my suitcase the thought was what do I take? How was I to choose? Which of my clothes, jewelry, computer, family pictures and then the most frightening thought of all, would it be for now, for a while or forever? The lights started to flicker. My family started to gather.

As I stood in front of the large bow window watching the majestic oaks and elm trees bend, reaching to the ground with their limbs as if for support, I realized we have absolutely no control. They looked like overcooked broccoli stalks limp on a fork. I remembered the tug-of-war between Mamma and my father. As children we learned to put the dog, needles, and scissors away from us as they were thought to be conductors of electricity and a bolt of lightning would find us. Out came Mamma's old folded up picture of God to which we prayed. We would recite "*Lampu e tronu sta luntanu, chista è la casa di lu nostru Diu.*" (Lighting and thunder stay away, this is the home of our God). My father would come along and invite us outside to see the bolts of lightning as they crackled across the sky. He would say, "When the lighting strikes begin to count one and two and until you heard the clap of thunder which was an indicator of how far away in miles the storm was.

We know that Super Storm Sandy destroyed parts of the landscape and seascape of Long Island forever. Those people directly affected with the loss of their home and possessions will recover to what extent? The question, "What happened?" will never have a clear answer. We will once again ask, "What is the purpose of life? And the only answer is "A life of purpose." For now we stand tall and begin to rebuild.

"The Mighty Oak"

For today, you are the mighty oak.
Put aside all the would have, could have and should have,
lay down your burdens for they can never be,

lift up your eyes and realize you are free,
free to breathe and laugh and love,
listen for the first chirped songs of spring.
Spring in your step, spring in your curl,
even spring in your mattress, will never be as glorious
as earth's spring:
a time of renewal, a time of rebirth.
Realize as a mighty oak, you have given shelter.
weathered the storm,
and now with tender buds ready to bloom into leaves,
you once again will start anew.
Lift up your roots and your brown bark skirt
and dance and praise, for now you are still
"The Mighty Oak"

A Sicilian proverb: "*Sia scantu, sia nenti, quannu si cunta.*" Being scared is nothing as long as we can talk about it. . .

Anna and Lorenzo
A Timeless Romance

Literature gives us a magnificent play – *Romeo and Juliet* – with two young lovers whose passions are so deep, whose beings and spirits are so entwined, that one cannot live without the other.

In life, our family and friends had Anna and Lorenzo. The morning was bright and beautiful. The town square was bustling with peddlers. Anna was there with her mother and sisters. Today was her fifteenth birthday. Mamma promised her a tortoise shell hair comb. Lorenzo and his friends were passing through the small town of Castelvetrano in the province of Trapani, Sicily. He was on holiday from the university in Rome. They planned to stay just the night. The town square was crowded and Lorenzo turned and collided with Anna. He excused himself and, with great flair, asked her mother's forgiveness and permission to speak to Anna. He looked at her breathlessly. When asked by anyone how she appeared, he would say he saw a young sparrow – slender in stature with the face of an angel and dark, dark eyes. Her eyes mesmerized him. He felt as though he was falling into the midnight sky, filled with twinkling stars. Her head was covered with a million curls that spilled onto her face. He could feel her blood surging through his veins.

She would then tell us that the moment she saw him, he completed her. He was tall, olive-skinned with eyes that were like pools of liquid caramel that reflected her. When he spoke, his words sounded like poetry. Eloquent both in speech and mannerisms, he took her breath away. She felt his heart beating in her breast. In her world, there would be no other. With her mother Donna Rosina's permission, he spent his holiday in town. Seeing Anna as much as he could, he was never happier. Soon, Lorenzo's friends returned. Holiday was over and they had to return to Rome.

The young lovers were sad. They said their goodbyes and promised their love to each other. Lorenzo assured her that when he returned, he would take her as his wife and they would live together forever.

Upon returning to Rome's train station, the young men were met by their manservants and whisked away. Lorenzo entered his family's palatial estate. The massive front doors opened onto a great room filled with marble floors, gilded mirrors and furniture from the four corners of the earth. Lorenzo raced up the sweeping staircase. With great excitement, he told his parents of his plans to marry. With horrified looks upon their faces, the most chilling words that he would ever hear left their lips. "No – you will not marry a poor, uneducated Sicilian girl. She will never be accepted by us or our friends. If you disobey us, you will be disinherited and your support at the university will end. See if she would want you then. No longer will you be called our son."

Italians and Sicilians would become crazed at the thought of losing face. From childhood, Lorenzo's family had planned for him to marry Emilia, a girl from a very wealthy and well-connected family. To Lorenzo's family, losing face would mean that they had lost all control over their son's decisions. They would feel the wrath of Emilia's family, who would assume she was not good enough for Lorenzo. His family would be disgraced and would no longer be included in the high society of Rome. This was their darkest day. They demanded that Lorenzo stay one more year at the university. He was enraged at the assumption that Anna was of no value and must have bewitched him. Only out of respect for all his parents had done for him, he agreed. His parents were elated and expected that once he was in the throes of study and social events, he soon would announce his engagement to Emilia. Both families in Rome immersed him in the wondrous life he would have as a successful doctor. Lorenzo suffered in silence at the many jokes and whispered innuendos of the seductive Sicilian girl with special powers in keeping his heart and mind imprisoned. Lorenzo's father said that Anna was someone to be enjoyed for the summer and remembered as a fling when he was an old man.

Days turned into weeks and weeks into months. Anna, having heard not a word, became melancholy and frail. She said to mamma, "I feel like a bird with a broken wing. I want to fly to Lorenzo, but even in my dreams I try and lose my breath. I fear he must be sick or dead. He would not stay away this long without a letter or a visit." In Sicily, life was filled with relatives, countrymen, even strangers that carried messages from Africa, all parts of Italy, and even as far away as America. Lorenzo remained a mystery. Now convinced he had broken his promise, she became very ill. In desperation, mamma called Doctor Campanella. He said she had developed an infection throughout her body. He prescribed medicine, bed rest, and only chicken broth to sustain her. The money was scarce. Mamma had been left to raise Anna, Vincenza, Angelina and Vincenzo who at age nine, was already an apprentice to a bricklayer. Her husband's money arrived from America where he labored on the railroad and slept on a hot bed. This was a mattress on the floor that was used by the men on a twenty-four hour rotation shift. Times were hard on both sides of the ocean.

The doctor said chicken broth was all that Anna could digest, so mamma agreed and chickens she bought. She cooked the chickens and served Anna the broth. Vincenza and Angelina, Anna's little sisters, danced round and round, filling their senses with the wondrous smells. They were reminded of *Carnevale*, a feast when meat was served. As they twirled, their smiling faces turned to masks of horror as they watched their mother throw the chicken away. Horrified, they screamed "Mamma, Mamma! Why are you doing that? We are so hungry!" Startled, Mamma turned with sadness and eyes overflowing with tears and tried to explain. "When you cook for a sick person, you cook with sadness and prayers, so that the food will nourish only that person. No one else should feel the sorrow and pain." The girls hugged their mother and said, "Don't be sad. We will pray harder for Anna."

A week passed and the doctor returned. Examining Anna he said, "Signora Rosina, the infection has spread and I fear that she most likely will not be able to bear a child." The news was devastating. Mother and daughter fell into each other's arms and cried. The sobs were heard by the neighbors, who knocked on the door to ask what had happened. Mamma whispered to Anna that no one was to know and that this heartache should never be discussed again. As time went on, Anna regained her health. A year had gone by and summer would soon be upon them. Sitting outside with her eyes down, she worked on her trousseau — with stitches so small, her designs looked like a drawing. She saw a tall shadow at her feet. Her heart raced. She lifted her eyes and saw Pietro, Lorenzo's friend. Pietro explained to Anna what Lorenzo felt he must do. Being a dutiful son, he would once again tell his parents of his intentions to marry Anna and beg them to be part of his new life. When Lorenzo tried to explain to his parents, his mother and father, stone-faced and as cold as ice, said, "We have wondered all these years when and if you would return to your birth's motherland." Lorenzo knew he was adopted, and had never felt the unconditional love he felt with Anna and her family. They said their goodbyes and he left as he had arrived – a stranger, a little boy lost.

Anna's days went by slowly with the anticipation of his return. She prayed to the Holy Father: "Holy Father, you spared me from death and returned me to health; help me become his wife." At that moment, saying the word wife, she was frozen in thought. *How will I tell him of my illness and impossibility of having a child?* It was August. It was a beautiful sunny day; Anna was sixteen years old. A rapid knock on the door sounded – and there he was. They embraced and cried tears of joy and sorrow and vowed never to be apart again. He asked for her hand in marriage. Before she answered, Anna cried and told him of the cross God asked them to bear. Lifting her face and moving the tear-filled curls while looking deeply into her eyes, he said, *"per sempre tu sei la mia vita"* (for always, you are my life).

Now, as a husband to-be, he needed a job. As a rich young man, study was his work. His every need was met by servants and caretakers. He had truly lived *la bella vita* (a beautiful life). Becoming an apprentice at nineteen years old was unheard of. Vincenzo introduced him to his *mastru* (the bricklayer instructor). Lorenzo worked for several days. His hands became raw and bleeding. Every night, Anna would beat egg whites and lovingly put them on his hands to relieve the pain. She ripped the pillowcases she had reserved for her wedding to make bandages for his hands. Drying her tears, he assured her "we are young and in love. That's all that matters." He kissed her softly and said since coming back to her, he no longer had the reoccurring dream of being a little boy lost with no one to hold his hand.

Several other back-breaking jobs proved disastrous. Out of respect for Donna Rosina, the neighbors continued to recommend him for various occupations. As a fisherman, he turned green with the roll of the sea and the smell of the fish. As a farmhand, the heavy lifting and constant digging left him with a hunched back and bug bites in places he was embarrassed to scratch. He marveled at the friendships extended to him. He was always welcome to drink and enjoy a meal with the men. Each encouraged him; "Life is to be lived — enjoy your love and tomorrow the sun will shine brighter."

In Rome, as a scholar, he was respected and never questioned. His father's philosophy: *un uomo intelligente lavora con la mente – solamente un asino lavora con le spalle* (an intelligent man works with his mind – only a jackass works with his shoulders). Lorenzo regretted having believed this when he overheard a man call him *mischinu* – a word reserved for a poor, wretched, miserable man of weak mind and body. The man continued, "This boy does not know how to do anything (*stu picciottu nun sapi fari nenti.*" Fate, *La forza del destino* had brought him here to this speck on the world's map. Here, you needed to be smart of mind and strong of body. He vowed to become both.

And then, one Sunday morning, there was a knock at the door.

The door opened and they were surprised to see *signor* Franco, the town's esteemed barber. Lorenzo rose and welcomed him in. The old barber said he had prayed that someone would come and take his place. His dream was to return to his beloved mountain home that he had left at age seven to become an apprentice. "It would be my honor, Lorenzo, if you would choose my profession," he said. Lorenzo looked at Anna and, together, they said "yes." Mamma looked at them both and said, "If you were birds, you would have been caught in the same cage." *Signor* Lorenzo, the new barber, was soon embraced by all. He learned quickly. His mannerisms, quick wit, intelligence and knowledge of politics, world travel and medicine were sought after. Barbers (*li varveri*) acted as doctors, applying leeches, lancing boils and working with skin diseases. Lorenzo finally felt useful and proud of himself. Travelers, townspeople and gossip flowed through the shop.

Lorenzo and Anna would now be married. He was now a man with a respected profession. Their wedding was a simple gathering of friends, neighbors and Anna's family. As they exchanged their vows, she could hear the angels sing. Pietro, a true friend, was the best man. No word came from Lorenzo's family. After the festivities of the wedding, they traveled to the seashore for holiday. While there, Anna noticed a *zingara*, a gypsy, who told fortunes. Excited, she said that she wanted to know their future. She gazed into her eyes and said she knew all she needed to know. The fortune teller took her hand and said, "Your love for each other will never end. You will live long and prosperous lives. Your hearts beat as one and your blood flows within each other. But, when one dies, the other will follow. There shall be two children – a boy and a girl. You are not the mother. They will always be with you and you will love them as if they are your own."

A few years passed and word came to Mamma. Papa wrote that it was time to bring the family to America. Anna said she would die without her mother, and so they all made plans to move. Mamma and Anna moved into their own apartments in the same building at 224 Bushwick Avenue in Brooklyn. Anna worked as a seamstress and Lorenzo continued as a barber. His talent and personality preceded him. He was known as a first-class man (*uomo di classe*). Customers filled his new shop. He was now *il padrone*.

Anna and Lorenzo, saving their money, were soon able to purchase a six-family building on Bushwick Avenue in the Bushwick section of Brooklyn. This was considered a great achievement for a young couple.

The façade was brown stone with oak doors that held leaded glass windows. When Anna was asked what her secret to this great achievement was, she simply said, "*si sarva la farina quannu la maidda è china* (you save the flour when the trough is full)." Another of her favorite proverbs was "*si stenni lu pedi quantu lu linzolu teni*" (stretch your foot only as far as your sheet covers). She would say, "If you remember these two proverbs, you will always have what you want."

Her new home had a beautiful, black wooden banister, a tiled bathroom and a kitchen large enough for a dining room set. Her living room sofa and chairs were burgundy and gold velvet. An exotic, oriental rug covered the dark, oak floors. She was determined to surround Lorenzo with the most unique treasures imported from Italy. The large front window was removed to allow a magnificent, black, shiny player piano to be brought into the house. Frank and I marveled at the pulleys and ropes that hoisted the piano to her second floor and through the window. We looked forward to being the first to pump our feet and make beautiful music. The piano was not complete without a handsome stuffed pheasant on top. Frank and I were fascinated by the iridescent feathers on its neck. We lovingly called him, "Charlie."

At family gatherings, everyone remarked when in their presence that they could feel the couple's love. Once she was asked, "Anna, when you look at Lorenzo, what do you see?" She simply answered, "Pluck my eyes and look through them and then you will see what I see." Lorenzo was asked, "Have you not gotten tired of holding her in the palm of your hand?" He responded with a smile and a wink at Anna, "No, never." "Are you sorry you gave up the riches of Rome?" He would say, "No, now I have the riches of the world." At parties, they danced as if they were one. With his fingers firmly pressed on the small of her back, they waltzed through life.

One day at a holiday gathering as I sat on Anna's lap, an acquaintance remarked to her, "you hold your sister's children so tight to your side and look at them adoringly — as if they were yours." She replied, "I did not bear them, but they are in my heart. If they needed the last drop of my blood, I would gladly give it to them." She continued to tell the women about the vision the *zingara* had so many years before. They quickly gathered, for this was the first time she spoke of her inability to have children. She confessed that she often dreamed of adoption, but the thought of the child abandoning her and Lorenzo brought too much sadness to her heart. Lorenzo's abandonment at birth, and by his adoptive parents, was incomprehensible to them both.

They lived a long and happy life. As the years passed, Anna developed a heart condition. Lorenzo was devastated and treated her like a doll made from sugar, afraid that she would break at any moment. She held his hand and reassured him constantly: "I will never leave you." As life continued, he suffered a stroke. The doctor suggested she get help to care for him. At that moment, with newfound strength and the prowess of a lioness protecting her young, she said there would be no need for that. She welcomed friends and relatives to keep him engaged in life, play checkers and talk about politics – all the things that he enjoyed. She continually reassured him that all would be well. Daily, she lit a candle in front of Saint Anthony, her patron saint. One day I asked, "Why do you pray to Saint Anthony and not the Holy Father?" With a smile she said, "The Holy Father may be too busy to hear me, but I know Saint Anthony will carry my prayers to him." These were always the same: *please let me live to serve my husband and never let him feel abandoned again.*

Lorenzo, in his 80th year, died that fall. Anna was inconsolable. At the moment of his death, the color drained from her face. Her eyes became dull and lifeless. Sighs, tears and audible prayers were always on her lips. She wore her black mourning dress and stockings day in and day out. She refused the medicine given to her to ease her grief. She said she wanted – and needed – to feel the grief because Lorenzo deserved to be mourned. Her prayers now became: *Come Holy Father and take me, for now my life on earth is complete.* The weight she was losing, the food that remained uneaten and her broken heart were of great concern to us. The day of her doctor's appointment, she answered the door for me and Frank. She was dressed in her light-colored "going out" clothes. She ate breakfast and said with a smile that she was ready to go. Anna had an aura of peace around her. The doctor said, "She is willing herself to die; there is nothing we can do." Frank and I noticed that she became playful with our children and smiled when we went to see her.

Spring came and our *cara zia* left peacefully in her dreams.

The gathering of family and friends was joyful. Everyone felt privileged to have witnessed true love. The women remarked that even in their advanced years, Anna and Lorenzo openly proclaimed their love and desire for each other. They spoke of his fingers often lingering at the nape of her neck; of casual pauses as his hand patted her shoulder; even of the attention he paid to a curl blown by the wind. The women recalled how she would always find the teaspoon he liked best; how she would procure the cup from a matched set, rewashed and placed by his cloth napkin; how she made sure his clothes were always perfectly pressed. Anna's attention to every detail had amazed us. Her eyes smiled in his presence.

In thought, we could hear the angels sing and see the little boy — whom she called *Lorenzino* — and the little girl — whom he called *Ninuzza* — walking hand-in-hand up the sun-lit path of eternity.

And so they will remain, forever in our hearts with love.

Rustic Folklore

Short stories that have no historical value, they are meant to teach a life lesson.

Dear Mother

"*Cara matri* (dear mother), why do you cry?"

She said, "You are my only son, but you don't care. All my friends have good sons that bring them jewelry, furs, and money. I sit here poor and ashamed of you while you study and study some more. Someday I will be rich you promise, but not today."

"Mother, the boys you speak of hurt and rob innocent people."

"I don't care," she insisted. "Just take, take like the others do."

The young boy, not wanting his mother to be ashamed of him, began a life of crime. He brought her all that she wanted. The more he brought, the more she praised him and said how proud she was.

Soon the day came when he was arrested and put into jail. She covered her face so no one would recognize her and went to belittle and curse her son.

"I am ashamed of you, look what you have done to me. Everyone knows why you are behind bars."

The son called the mother over.

"Mama, mama, come closer. I want to kiss you and tell you I love you."

As she stepped close to the bars, he grabbed her by the ears and bit off her nose.

"You always told me to take, take," he said. "Now you will be ashamed of the way you look. If you had told me how wrong it was to rob others, neither one of us would be in this predicament."

*Proverb: *Lu nnuccenti chianci pri lu piccaturi* (the innocent cries for the sinner).

134

Donna Nella

Donna Nella was the landowner's wife. Wanting to be useful, she said to her husband, "I will go to town and pay all the bills." "No, no," said the husband. "This is a dangerous job and you are only a woman." "Only a woman, you say? I can outsmart all the men. I will carry the money where they won't be able to get it." Her husband warned her, "Dear wife, do not brag and tell no one. When you brag, someone will try to outsmart you." As usual, she did not listen.

Preparing to leave for town, she began to sing, "La la la, I will carry a gun and put the money *nta lu portafogghiu* (wallet)." Outside of her window, one of the young workers who thought himself to be a wise guy was listening. He had already made a bet with his friends and the ringleader that he was going to rob her. Laughing, the ringleader said, "And if you succeed, what will you want?" Thinking, the young wise guy said, "I want the honor of wearing the *coppula* (cap) the way you do." They agreed.

The young man enlisted the help of his friend Peppino and told him what to do. *Lu Patruni*'s wife went on her merry way. Walking under a large tree, she was shocked by a bucket of cold water which Peppino dumped on her head. Taken by surprise, she raised her arms above her head. The young wise guy quickly lifted her skirt, and thrust his hand in and retrieved the money from Donna Nella's *portafogghiu*.

Claiming his prize, he was now known as *Lu malandrinu di Palermu cu la coppula storta,* which means "The rogue from Palermo with the cocked cap."

Eggplants

Riding along a country road, an olive oil merchant came upon a farmer and his beautiful daughter. "Good day," he said.

Handing the papa a bottle of his finest olive oil, he stated his intentions. "I would like to romantically pursue your daughter." Mesmerized by the handsome oil, the farmer agreed.

The one-sided romance began. You see, she was madly in love with the farmhand. What could she do?

The merchant asked, "What gifts can I bring to you, my dear?" She responded, "Oil, lots and lots of oil, for I have a field of eggplants to fry." Each time the merchant came, he found her peeling, slicing the eggplant lengthwise, salting and pressing the slices into a colander to drain the bitterness.

Bottle after bottle of oil was used to make fried eggplant (*milingiani fritti*), crispy on the outside, and creamy soft on the inside. Platters piled high were sent to and enjoyed by the priest, nuns, and neighbors.

One day, the young farmhand came to make a delivery. The merchant noticed their dreamy eyes as she held his plump, hard, dark-skinned blemish-free rounded eggplants in her hands.

Soon the extra virgin olive oil was no more. Now, contentedly, the family enjoyed *caponata* instead.

*Story told with a wink and a smile.

Farmer Knows Best

Every morning, the farmer would say:

"*Campa sceccu ca l'erba crisci* (live donkey for the grass will grow)."

The poor donkey, whose ribs were starting to show, would nod his head and say,

"Hee-haw, hee-haw."

The old farmer would pray for rain so that the old donkey would have his fill of green grass. The day came when the donkey looked like he was taking his last breath. He said,

"*Basta*! Why do you say *campa sceccu*?"

The farmer said,

"*Unni c'è vita, c'è spiranza* (where there is life, there is hope)."

Encouraged, the donkey stood up, regained his strength and said,

"Hee-haw."

As they both prayed, it began to rain.

Garden Secrets

Gabriella, as a young bride, wanted to WOW her new husband. A vegetable garden was planted; *insalata* (salad), was his favorite part of *Lu Pranzu* (his dinner).

The tomatoes grew slowly, so the bride asked her neighbor, "How do you grow your tomatoes so big?" With finger to her lips and a quick look around, the old lady shared her secret. "In your naughty nighty, come out and dance in front of the tomatoes by the light of the *luna d'argentu* (silvery moon) and sing. For you, tomatoes, I sing and do this dance!"

Several days passed, the old woman looked over the fence and asked, "Did you do what I said?" "Yes," said the bride. "The tomatoes still don't want to grow, but did you ever see cucumbers this big?"

Told with a wink and a smile.

It Cannot Be

"No, it cannot be. You're mistaken," he said. "Even if an angel comes from heaven, I will not believe my beautiful wife is being unfaithful."

Lunchtime at the factory was like an active beehive, rife with laughter, finger pointing, and innuendos directed at Salvatore. He could take no more – he dropped his lunch and ran home. As usual, he rang the bell and knocked on the door. With his key, he entered and called her name.

"Francesca!"

She responded, "Here, in the bedroom. Quiet, please."

He entered and found his wife resting on the fluffed-up pillows with her hand on her brow and her bed sheet under her chin, moaning *"La testa mi fa mali!"* Salvatore began to look in the closet, behind the dresser and under the sheets. He said to his wife, "You have been unfaithful! The men at work said you were probably doing *la tirachitolla* while I worked hard." As she began to cry, he lifted the skirt of the bed and there was his *cumpari.*

And so the saying goes: *cu l'oocchi spirdati comu lu compari sutta lu lettu* (with his eyes wide as if he saw a spirit was the best man hiding under the bed). The best man beat the poor husband for coming home earlier than usual. And so he was *curnutu e bastuniatu* — he was not only made a fool of, but he was also beaten senseless.

Old Friends

There were two friends – one was frugal and one was not. A knock on the door and the friend that needed instant gratification was there.

"Dear friend," he said, "I must ask you for twenty dollars."

"Of course. There in the drawer you will find what you need. When you return the money, just put it in the drawer."

The twenty dollars was returned and borrowed many times. In and out of the drawer the money went and the friendship grew. One day, the friend came to borrow the twenty dollars. His friend, gracious as always, said,

"Sure, my friend; you know where the drawer is."

Opening the drawer, he found nothing. Angry, he said,

"There is no money in the drawer."

The frugal friend asked,

"Did you put the money back?"

"No," came the answer.

"Well," said the friend, "*zoccu si sarva si trova* (what you save is what you'll find). Only if you borrow and return it will you find it again."

Not only did he lose the twenty dollars, but he also lost a friend.

Moral of the story: money is a traitor.

Papa

"Papa, tomorrow we will leave early. I want to take you on a trip." Morning came and the old man, now feeble and sick prepared to leave. Riding in the cart, he turned, looking behind. He visualized the fields that had flourished under his care. His sweaty brow dried by the swaying branches and gentle breeze of the old mulberry tree. His ears were filled with his wife's laughter and sweet songs as he rocked the newborns on his knee.

As the cart's wheels rattled along the bumpy road, he noticed his son was preoccupied and filled with sadness. A father knows when a child has tried his best. Money, time, and fortitude had all failed his son.

Soon they came upon a large rock. "Papa," the son said, "you will rest on this rock under the sky and sun that you love, I will be back." Papa hugged his son and said, "I trust you." With many blessings, he waved goodbye. Weeks turn into months, months into years and soon into decades. The son, now the papa, was told to prepare for a motor trip. Old and feeble, he agreed. "Yes, my son, I will be ready."

As they approached the large rock, it was the father who said, "Here my son, I know this rock well, I will wait for your return, I trust you." "ADDIU".... What we do to others we can one day expect. (*Chi la fa, l'aspetta*)

Old age is a scoundrel - a robber of all things young.

Surprise - Surprise

Papa would always say, "Don't let me forget *la casciaforti* (strong box). I promise, whomever I'm with, gets the box."

Children, grandchildren, friends, and neighbors were always visiting or extending an invitation to Papa and Louisa.

One morning, Louisa woke up to find Papa *mortu*, dead. She looked in all the nooks and crannies of the house. The strong box was nowhere to be found. And soon neither was anyone else.

Time passed, Louisa prayed, "Dio, answer me, how can I get them all to come back?" As she prayed, she noticed a corner of the strong box peeking from under the now depleted wood pile.

Opening the box, she remained *"cu la vucca aparta"* (with her mouth open) at what she saw. Smiling, she quickly locked the box and notified everyone that she was making the same promise as Papa had made.

As if by magic, she was surrounded and invited by everyone. Accepting the invitations, she was reminded (don't forget the strong box.)

Attending a neighbor's wedding, she danced and danced and soon *bara-puffa-ti* (a Sicilian sound). Smiling, she fell dead.

La casciaforti broke open, everyone stood with their eyes and mouth wide open at what they saw.

Surprise! – Surprise!

Contented Man

"Papa, Papa, will I ever be contented?" Day in and day out the son lamented. Papa tried to explain, "Give of yourself, go fishing, look at the sea and sky and pray." Nothing helped.

Exasperated, the father said, "Go on a trip and find a contented man and ask to buy his undershirt and underwear and put them on."

His son soon left and traveled far and wide. From Palermo to Agrigento to Syracuse to Messina, he was not able to find a truly contented man. And then, finally, in Cefalù he found what he had been looking for. "*Signuri, Signuri!* Please I must buy your undershirt and underwear."

Laughing and dancing the man said, "I am not wearing any, I dance *friscu friscu* with the wind blowing where it wants."

The Engagement

Ah, la primavera, young lovers' hearts were all a flutter. This festive occasion, the engagement of Mario from Ragusa, and Rosaria from Milan, was being celebrated by friends and family. Mario, the hunter (*lu cacciaturi*), was well known and respected throughout the land. Proudly he took his seat at the head of the banquet table. On his right, his hunting dogs and his fiancée (*fidanzata*). On his left, his lifelong friend Antonio, and soon to be his best man (*lu cumpari*). He had introduced the lovers and was very fond of the bride-to-be.

Speeches, raised glasses that overflowed with wine, and well wishes were in abundance.

Mario soon realized that every time Rosaria yawned, Antonio did too. The other guests that yawned must also be in on this private signal, and soon to be a betrayal, he thought. As he extended his hand to caress hers, she quickly pulled her hand away to cover her yawn. "Basta, basta!" (enough), Mario said as he slammed his fist on the table, jumped up, reached for his shotgun and pointed it at his friend. As he began to speak, he lifted his hand to cover his mouth, as he too began to yawn. BOOM, shooting the chandelier, he quickly realized there had been no secret sign for infidelity, but instead a common occurrence. Yawns were indeed contagious.

The Princess

The palace was alive with happiness. The young prince had come home with a bride. Everyone was put on alert. She was to have all that her heart desired. Her ladies in waiting asked, "what are your desires, princess?"

Coming from a far away land, no one knew of her existence, who she was, or her family's lineage.

This beautiful, young creature with ringlets the color of chestnuts, eyes as dark as black figs that sparkled like her diamond tiara, and lips as red as cherries, was welcomed by all. Her request: chairs to be put into a circle in the lavish ballroom with one chair in the center, a basket of bread and one gold coin. Then she requested to be left alone for an hour or two each morning. The preparations were made and the doors were closed.

Outside, the servants gathered and listened as the princess in a sweet voice said "Please, Sir (*pi piaciri signuri*), perhaps you can spare a piece of bread for this poor girl?" "Please, Miss (*pi piaciri, signurina*), will you be so kind as to spare me some bread." The servants, tripping over each other, could not believe their eyes while peering through the keyhole. The princess approached the center chair. Taking the gold coin, she fluttered her eyelashes, giggled, and curtsied.

The prince came upon his servants unexpectedly. They clamored "Who is she? Where did she come from? Why is she begging?" Patiently, he explained he had given a gold coin to a street urchin who wore tattered clothes and was begging. His heart grew wings and he became transfixed on her adorable face. "The princess may never be comfortable with all her riches and will continue to beg. I ask that you respect who she is now and love her as I do."

*Proverb: *Attentu, la manu d'abbitudini è forti*. Careful, hand of a habit is strong.

145

The Sacristan

"*Gesù Cristu*, do you remember me from yesterday? I have returned today to pray for good weather."

Tuesday came and he was there again.

"Today I pray for those that have no shoes. *Gesù*, remember yesterday? I was here and I'm here again today. Every day I come to pray, and so I cannot work."

This continued for the rest of the week. Every day he came, and every day he prayed, and every day he blamed his prayers for keeping him from work.

"Everyone says go to work, but how can I when I have to pray to you, God?"

The sacristan, who worked very hard, was tired of hearing the man make excuses every day. In a booming voice, he yelled from behind the altar,

"It's time for you to go to work and pray!"

The man was startled. Glaring up at the cross, he said,

"You did not learn your lesson! Have you forgotten? Look at the trouble you got into because of your long tongue *(linguazza)*."

Where Is My Donkey?

"*Unu, dui, tri, quattru e cin...* one, two, three, four and..."

He never completed the number five.

You see, the story goes that the farmer was going into town to sell his five donkeys. Before sunrise, he fed and brushed his five donkeys. He led them out of their stalls and now was ready to leave. Again, he began to count. When he got to number five, he stopped. With anger and frustration, he yelled for his wife.

"Maria," he demanded, "did you take my fifth donkey?"

She began to laugh and, pointing at him, she said,

"*Hai lu sceccu sutta di tia e lu vai a circari* (you have the donkey under you and you are looking for it)."

Embarrassed, he went to town.

We were reminded of this story many times, whenever we lost a shoe, a wallet or a book that was hidden in plain sight. Sometimes, we were reminded that even love and happiness were right under our noses.

Young Man's Logic

"Dear nephew (*caru niputi*), I would like the privilege to take you out to dinner."

"*Caru ziu* (dear uncle), I am honored."

Now that the nephew was of age, the uncle wanted him to be prepared for adulthood. Fine dining and manners were most important. Uncle ordered the best steak and finest wine. The steaks arrived on a silver platter. Uncle said,

"Nephew, you go first."

The platter held one steak that was slightly smaller than the other. Now to see if the nephew had proper manners.

The nephew took the largest steak and passed the platter to his uncle. Immediately, the uncle raised a finger and said,

"Tsk, tsk! Nephew, you have manners to learn."

"Why, Uncle?"

"Well, you see, when offered a platter of meat, you always take the smaller piece."

"If the platter was given to you first, uncle, which would you have taken?"

Uncle, without hesitation, said,

"The small one, of course."

The nephew smiled and said,

"And so I would have gotten the big steak anyway?"

The uncle thought for a moment, raised his glass and said,

"A toast — to a young man's logic!"

Life's Quilt

Thought provoking ideas:

you're born alone and you will die alone.

No one is put on this earth to make you happy.

True happiness comes from within, nourish it.

Life unfolds as to the choices you make.

My father believed and lived by these words, as do I,

repeating them often to family and friends.

Life like a patchwork quilt, that when held close brings you warmth, or as you wrap yourself, you're filled with guilt that someone else is cold.

Do you surround yourself in anger, sadness, or unachieved wishes?

You sometimes look around with envy at the many quilts, made of woven threads of gold, fabrics of velvet, and silk.

Others we see, live their life with a quilt that's threadbare, mis-stitched, and soiled, thinking that's all I am worth.

Is this attitude learned, self taught, believed or inherited?

Why can some rise above adversity, poverty or infirmity, while many voluntarily fall to the ground to be stomped and spat upon?

It is said that we choose our births' circumstances.

The path we walk is to learn to redo what we did wrong, to complete the unfinished.

Sins repented will bring us glory.

We are all human and that's where all similarity ends.

As I see it, we have one constant denominator: 24 hours in a day.

How we spend it, is our own struggle.

When I was young I feared death.

As I age, I fear life, its uncertainties, suffering, and the changing

149

landscape where pebbles have become boulders. But, for today I silence my mind, open my heart, and bask in the sunlight of family and friends, wrapped with love in my quilt called "Life".

Sicilian Life Beyond the Veil

Imagine the biblical account of the day when Salomé performed the Dance of the Seven Veils. Salomé's mother was now married to King Herod. It seems, as the story goes, that she was disrespected by John the Baptist. She asked Salomé to dance for the King as a gift for his birthday with the intention of requesting that her daughter ask the King for the head of John the Baptist on a platter. The dance was very seductive with the King giving into his manly wiles and leaving him with incestuous desire. The veils were slowly removed as the dance continued until the King was so enamored and exhausted that he agreed to her request.

Veils represent the illusion of things seen and not seen, things imagined and those that are unimaginable. The mourning veil was worn by many widows so that their head was covered in church and they could hide their crying eyes from view. A white bridal veil has a protective function; it hides the bride from evil spirits, or anyone with the evil eye until the wedding ritual begins.

Many Sicilians left their homeland with the intention of abandoning their parents and family, changing their names so that they could now blend with other cultures. Coming to America and living in the tenements forced many to live beyond the veil. One face was shown to friends and relatives until their doors were closed. Unfortunately, the walls were so thin and they lived so close to each other that lust, abuse, and all things human were heard by their neighbors. Gossip was spread here and back in the old country.

The veil of secrecy was the call for fraternities and brotherhoods with death as the only path to liberation. We have often heard, pull aside the veil, lift the veil, and look through the veil. These all conjure up our own perception of the forbidden.

The phenomenon of a baby being born with a veil, a transparent skin that covered only the face was rarely seen. They truly lived beyond the veil. *La Mammana*, the midwife, told my grandmother Cecelia that her son was such a phenomenon. The veil was removed and saved. These children are known to be visionaries, sensitive, and mystical healers. Whenever she spoke of this in front of her sons, she said that they were all special. We noticed she would pause as she looked at one of them. He will remain beyond the veil. In all cultures this skin is sought after, especially by sailors that feel the need to be protected against drowning.

All that's left is to be brave and lift whatever veil that may be clouding our vision of the great beyond.

FOR NOW I SAY, THANK YOU FOR YOUR COMPANY ON THIS JOURNEY. UNTIL WE MEET AGAIN . . . . ARRIVEDERCI.